BEAUTY
SLEEP

MICHAELE G. BALLARD

St. Martin's Paperbacks

TABLE OF CONTENTS

BEAUTY
SLEEP

ONE

April 10, 2001

It was considered routine plastic surgery.

Sandra Joyner was scheduled to have a mini-facelift, liposuction and fat grafts to fill in a couple of scars on her face and plump up her lips. While she was under, she decided to have her lower eyelids resurfaced to smooth out the tiny lines that had begun to form.

At 45, Sandra was still a beauty. She was a striking blonde, 5 feet 6 inches tall, and a toned and taut 115 pounds. But her life had fallen apart. She and John, her high school sweetheart and only real boyfriend, married after college and had two children. In 1999, after eighteen years of marriage, they had separated. Sandra's family had been her life, and now she was struggling to find her own identity. She thought the surgery would make her look more rested and help her to feel better about herself in general.

Her only job experience had been teaching high school, and she hadn't worked since her now teenaged sons were born. It was difficult enough trying to get a job without any marketable skills, but even more daunting was the singles scene. Sandra hadn't been single since she was 17 years old, and dating in 2000 at 45 was very different from dating as a high school student in the 1970s.

Sandra's parents and sister, with whom she had always been close, were not happy about her decision to have plastic surgery; they didn't understand why she thought she needed it. She had always been incredibly pretty and popular. In fact, she had been the belle of the ball wherever she went.

Sandra's estranged husband, John, who was paying for the surgery, saw no harm in it if she felt it would boost her self-esteem. Besides, the same doctor had completed a minor surgery on one of her eyes a couple of years earlier and she had been delighted with the results.

Sandra scheduled her appointment for 7 a.m., Tuesday, April 10, at the Center for Plastic and Cosmetic Surgery. It was only twenty-five minutes from the upscale South Charlotte apartment where she had been living by herself since separating from her husband the previous June.

Sandra was up early, around 5:30 a.m., but there wasn't much to do, since she couldn't wear makeup and wasn't allowed to eat or drink after midnight. All she had to do was brush her teeth, shower and run a brush through her shoulder-length, highlighted hair. She decided to wear jeans, a lightweight sweater and casual flats so she would be comfortable. It was early spring and the temperature would eventually hit 70 degrees, but at 6:15 a.m. the air was chilly. Sandra had been cold-natured all her life, so she threw on a light jacket at the last minute.

Around 6:20 a.m. she called a taxicab to take her to the center at 300 Billingsley Road. The night before, John had offered to take her to the appointment, but she told him that her mother and sister were taking her. To this day John has no idea why Sandra decided to take a cab to her appointment. He never found out if it was because her family had bowed out at the last minute, if they were going to pick her up after the surgery, or if she had simply lied to him about who was taking her. Regardless, it was odd that she went to the appointment alone, since she had a lot of close friends who would have been happy to accompany her.

The trip took longer than expected due to rush hour traffic. Dr. Peter Tucker, the plastic surgeon, and his nurse anesthetist, Sally Hill, had everything ready when Sandra arrived a few minutes late.

Sandra hadn't slept well the night before. In spite of taking a mild tranquilizer to help her sleep, she'd tossed and turned throughout the night. Admittedly she was feeling a little nervous about the surgery, and was more talkative than usual as she went through the pre-surgery procedures.

While Sally checked Sandra's vitals—her temperature, blood pressure and heart rate—Sandra rattled on about the traffic and her unproductive job search. She had just missed out on a job that she'd really wanted with US Airways, and felt sure it was because the company wanted someone younger. She also confided in Sally that she was going through a nasty divorce.

Sally had her own set of problems. Her marriage was on the rocks, too, and a year before, she'd been diagnosed with leukemia. But she always managed to put personal problems aside, to be a professional on the job. She had always been focused on her nursing career and took pride in her accomplishments. That day all Sandra's vital signs were normal except her hemoglobin, which had been tested a week earlier. It was a little low—11.5 ccs instead of 13—but when Sally mentioned it to the doctor, he didn't seem concerned. To Sandra's knowledge she was not allergic to any medications, so no additional allergy testing was done prior to the surgery.

At one point during her pre-operative check, Sandra became visibly apprehensive about going under the knife, as if questioning whether she was doing the right thing. This is not uncommon when patients are under stress, and

Sally reassured her, telling her there was nothing to worry about.

More than 11 million cosmetic procedures are performed every year in the U.S., which makes plastic surgery almost as common as teeth whitening. In addition, the chance that anything serious will go wrong is incredibly small. Besides, Sandra had every confidence in Dr. Tucker, who had corrected her drooping eye just two years earlier. She'd done her homework before deciding to have the surgery performed by Dr. Tucker: He came highly recommended by several people, and he had a framed award hanging in his office saying he was voted "Best Plastic Surgeon." However, there was no information available about how that choice was made, or by whom.

In 1999, Sandra had breezed through the procedure and post-operative recovery without a hint of a complication. Even more important, she had been very pleased with the results.

Sally had been a Certified Registered Nurse Anesthetist (CRNA) since 1982, and worked for the Presbyterian Hospital system for ten years in that capacity. It was there she first began working with Dr. Tucker.

Tucker and Sally had left the hospital system together when he became the third partner in an established plastic surgery office, then she'd gone with him when he decided to start his own practice in 1997. They had worked together on thousands of plastic surgery procedures without incident. In fact, Sally had been the nurse anesthetist on duty for Sandra's earlier surgery in 1999.

Although no one realized it, Sally and Sandra had known each other casually when they were young. They had attended the same elementary school and junior high, and at Olympic High School in the early 1970s, they'd run in the same crowd and had even gone out with the same boy at one point, although the girls weren't close friends.

Now assisting on Sandra's second procedure, Sally walked Sandra through the surgical process, turned on the oxygen and began to hook up the blood pressure machine, pulse oximeter and EKG monitor just as Dr. Tucker came into the room suited up in his green surgical scrubs, as he did almost every morning.

A personable man, Dr. Tucker stepped over to Sandra and patted her on the arm, assuring her that there was nothing to be concerned about, she would be happy with the final results.

At 7:30 a.m., Dr. Tucker gave Sandra a mild tranquilizer and Sally started the IV that would dispense the anesthetic and an antibiotic, which was customary during surgery to prevent any type of infection from occurring.

Dr. Tucker estimated that it would take three or four hours to complete all four of the scheduled procedures, barring any unforeseen complications.

He started with the mini-facelift, since it would be the most time-consuming and intricate of the four. First he did one side, then the other, which took a little over one and a half hours. One advantage to a mini-facelift is that there is a faster recovery period, since it is not as invasive as a full facelift, which requires larger incisions and heavier stitching. It is the perfect solution for baby boomers who just want to take five years off their faces, so they look like younger versions of themselves.

Next Dr. Tucker harvested a small amount of fat to mix with a commercial filler product and filled in a couple of scars on Sandra's face, and plumped up her lips.

Using laser therapy, he smoothed out lines around Sandra's eyes caused by the environment, crinkles that Sandra thought made her look tired all the time.

The mini-facelift and laser resurfacing were meant to give Sandra a more youthful and rested appearance, not to change her natural good looks. Three and a half hours later, all the work was completed and everything had gone as planned.

By 11:15 a.m. Sandra was on her way to the recovery room, where she would rest for a couple of hours before going home. She was groggy from the anesthesia, but was able to get into a wheelchair on her own for the short ride down the hall to the recovery area.

Before leaving the operating room, Sandra's vital signs were checked: Her blood pressure was 109/93; her pulse 99; respiration 16, and O_2 saturation was 96 percent, all of which were normal. Her skin was warm to the touch and pinkish in color.

Sandra talked to the nurses while they got her settled into the oversized recovery room recliner that was hooked up to monitoring devices. A technician covered her with a lightweight blanket and carefully placed ice packs on her bandaged face and swollen eyes.

Within minutes Sandra complained that her face hurt.

Technically, the nurse anesthetist's job was finished. Once a patient was in the recovery room Sally was supposed to go to the waiting area to get the next patient. But this particular day, the recovery room nurse asked Sally to watch the patients. It was part of the recovery room nurse's responsibility to check the patients' vital signs every fifteen minutes and document them on their charts while they were in recovery. Of course the nurse would also observe the patient to make sure there were not any changes in her condition. If there was any change, the nurse was supposed to alert the doctor immediately.

Sally, who had been diagnosed with leukemia and undergone chemotherapy a year earlier, had gained a lot of weight because of her treatment and lack of exercise. She seemed to like working in recovery—quite possibly because she didn't have to make as many trips up and down the hall to the waiting room. Sally said she often volunteered to help out so others could take a break, in spite of the fact that she had recently been chastised by the Chief CRNA for staying in the recovery room too long when that was not part of her job. The supervisor also reminded her that she should not give medication in the recovery room without the doctor's permission and she should always document all medications on the patients' records.

"My face hurts. It feels like it's on fire," a restless Sandra had complained almost immediately as she tried to get out of the recliner.

The level of pain was not surprising considering the amount of work that had been done on Sandra's face. By this time the anesthetic used in the IV was also beginning to wear off. Around 11:20 a.m., Sally stepped into the hall where she kept her supply cart and retrieved a syringe, and gave Sandra 1 cc of fentanyl, a fast-acting painkiller, intravenously.

At first the fentanyl seemed to calm Sandra, but within minutes she complained that it wasn't helping. By then, she had begun to draw her knees up to her chest in pain.

"Am I being a bad patient?" Sandra asked.

"No, of course not," Sally reassured her.

Five minutes after the first fentanyl, Sally administered another 1 cc dose for the pain. Both injections were given without consulting the doctor.

When the staff knew they would be in a long surgery, or had back-to-back procedures, they would step into the break room to get a quick bite to eat—a bagel or some yogurt, for instance—since there wouldn't be time for anything more. It was during one such instance, when Sally had stepped out of the recovery room for some coffee and a biscuit, that a certified surgical technician (CST) who happened to walk through the recovery room glanced at the monitor and saw the number 38. She feared that it might be the patient's heart rate. Then she noticed that Sandra's color had changed—her lips looked blue.

At first the CST wasn't alarmed; she thought the discoloration might be due to the fat grafts done on Sandra's lips, which could have easily bruised them. But when she walked around to the other side of the recliner to take a closer look, the nurse saw that Sandra's fingernails were also blue.

She went over and patted Sandra, calling her name as she tried to get a response, but there was none. She pinched Sandra's toe and called out "Sandra," again trying to get her to respond.

About that time the recovery room nurse walked back in and asked Sally, who had just returned, if Sandra was OK.

"She's fine," Sally replied.

The recovery room nurse pushed the recliner back and asked one of the CSTs to put the oxygen mask on Sandra.

"Take a deep breath," the nurse urged.

Sandra responded instantly, so the recovery room nurse walked out again.

Then—after seeing Sally go into the other room and come out of the OR and get something from her supply cart when she should have been watching the patient— she was asked if everything was all right.

"Do you want someone to get Dr. Tucker?" a surgical nurse asked, since the doctor was supposed to be notified any time there was a change in a patient.

"I have more than enough help," Sally reportedly said.

Sally was going about her business as calmly as she always did. There was no sense of urgency as she got a pre-mixed syringe of Robinul, to regulate the heart, and ephedrine to open the bronchical tubes if there were breathing difficulties. Sally always kept Robinul/ephedrine ready, just in case. Still there was no change in Sandra's condition.

The second time the recovery room nurse walked back in, she immediately noticed that Sandra's O_2 saturation and blood pressure had dropped. The blood pressure cuff and pulse oximeter monitors had been turned on when Sandra first arrived in the recovery room, but for some reason the alarm had not signaled that anything was wrong. Regardless, it was apparent Sandra's condition had deteriorated, so the recovery room nurse went next door immediately to get Dr. Tucker.

Dr. Tucker ran to the recovery room to find the staff hovering over Sandra; Sally met him at the door, but co-workers said she had been standing at the back of the room, doing nothing to help.

The air was thick, as if everything was happening in slow motion.

Dr. Tucker immediately began to intubate Sandra. But there was no change. He did compressions on her chest. His heart pounding, he yelled at the staff to get Sandra on the floor so he could use the paddles to revive her.

Still no change.

"Do you want me to call 911?" the recovery room nurse asked.

"Yes!" Dr. Tucker yelled.

Just twenty minutes earlier Sandra had seemed fine after being wheeled into the recovery room after her surgery. Now she was being rushed to the nearest medical facility, Mercy Hospital. En route, paramedics administered Narcan, a drug used to counteract the effects of an overdose of pain medication.

Once at the hospital a team of doctors worked feverishly

on Sandra, trying to revive her. One of the nurses called Sandra's mother and sister, who were listed as emergency contacts on Dr. Tucker's consent form.

There have been complications, the nurse told them. That was the only information they had when they arrived at the hospital.

For the remainder of the day the doctors ran batteries of tests, including MRIs and brain scans, trying to find any signs of life. That night, around 10 p.m., after working on Sandra nonstop since noon, a grim-looking doctor met with the family in a private room.

"There is nothing more we can do for her. Sandra stopped breathing after the second injection of fentanyl, and she lapsed into a coma," the doctor told them.

In simple terms, Sandra was brain-dead, a diagnosis that was later confirmed by two isoelectric (flat-line) EEGs, twenty-four hours apart, that indicated that the end of all brain activity was irreversible. There was no clinical evidence of brain activity, her organs were merely being kept alive by life support equipment.

Five days later, on Easter Sunday, April 15, the family gave the hospital permission to remove Sandra from the machines that were technically keeping her alive. She died not long afterwards.

Following an autopsy, the medical examiner determined that Sandra had died from an overdose of a painkiller thought to be fentanyl. She had gone into respiratory arrest and stopped breathing.

While tragic, it was considered a terrible accident, and there would be no need for a police investigation.

TWO

Early 70s: High School Days

Charlotte, North Carolina, was experiencing growing pains in the early 1970s, long before it would become one of the largest financial centers in the country and home to an impressive list of Fortune 500 companies. In fact, in the early 1970s there were only a handful of office buildings and one skyscraper downtown, which in Charlotte is referred to as *uptown*—perhaps because it has a more positive ring to it, and Charlotte has always been very concerned about image. Charles Kuralt, who grew up in Charlotte, was a master at telling stories about regular folks in the area, youngsters who still said "Yes, ma'am" out of respect for their elders, and Southerners who made award-winning sweet tea. He loved to show the rest of the country what they could expect when they went to a "pig pickin'" a gathering where a whole pig is roasted on a spit.

Charlotte, the largest city in North Carolina, is beautiful and well-kept. In fact, it has been said that "Charlotte is beautiful in a way that few cities can rival." In the springtime big oaks form a canopy over the older neighborhoods, cherry blossoms and dogwoods line the streets and pink and white azaleas bloom along the walkways. The downtown area is always well groomed with seasonal flowers, adding life to the office towers; older neighborhoods (many historical) are quaint, and the newer communities that are filled with multimillion-dollar homes are pristine.

Earlier in its development the city's population was made up mostly of people who worked at the textile mills, or farmers whose families worked the land for generations.

In 1799 Conrad Reed stumbled upon a seventeen-pound gold nugget while wading in a stream in a nearby town. Years later that same stream yielded a larger gold nugget, that one, at twenty-eight pounds, the largest ever found in the U.S. As word spread, farmers were soon hurrying through their chores so they could search for gold. Charlotte became the mining capital of the country. But by 1861 all the mines were boarded up and everyone headed West in the California Gold Rush.

Charlotte's central location between the cities of the Northeast and the agricultural lands of the South turned the area from a cotton producer to a thriving textile center bolstered by tobacco, furniture and corn "likker" (white lightnin' or moonshine). NASCAR, in fact, was born from the need for drivers to get white lightnin' off the mountain and to the buyers before law enforcement could catch them.

In the 1970s and 1980s, the town with big-city ideas, nicknamed The Queen City in honor of Queen Charlotte of Mecklenburg, wife of King George III of the United Kingdom, was just beginning to get noticed as a banking center. Today it is a major financial center and headquarters to Bank of America and Wachovia bank.

Sports were also a growing part of Charlotte's culture, and included the NASCAR racing circuit, the Charlotte Hornets basketball team (until 2003), playing host to the CIAA and NCAA tournaments year after year, and later the Charlotte Knights baseball team and Carolina Panthers football team. It was also home to sixteen-time wrestling champion "Nature Boy," Ric Flair.

In the early 70s the movers and shakers had begun to put emphasis on building the Charlotte–Mecklenburg school system—the largest in the state—into a model for quality education. Olympic and Independence High Schools were built at the same time in 1966, and having two new schools go up simultaneously was an important first for the city.

Olympic High, where Sandra and Sally attended their last years of public school, sat on what had been farmland owned by four or five families. In the school's first years there were only 700 students in grades 9 through 12. But by the mid-70s enrollment had doubled, partially due to court-ordered busing of students from lower Steele Creek, Dalton Village (a housing project) and Starmount. These children were shuttled to the new school in southeast Charlotte in order to ensure that the guidelines being imposed throughout the South, dictating that 70 percent of the students be white and 30 percent black, were met.

In addition to standard subjects, the school curriculum included cosmetology, carpentry, auto mechanics and brick masonry, a reflection of the area's blue-collar population. "But we did turn out one attorney, a doctor and a couple of politicians," added the coach, a longtime city councilman and later head of the school district.

"Olympic High was one of the smallest and one of the poorest schools," said Coach Joe White, who was the first head coach and athletic director at the school. "The Big O," as he dubbed it, was constantly trying to raise money to purchase athletic equipment, but in the end the school's staff, including Coach White, generally had to help buy the equipment out of their own pockets. "We didn't even have our own athletic field," said White. "We had to play football at Myers Park High School. I often said we played more games at Myers Park than they did."

For the Friday night games, everyone would pile into

friends' or parents' cars to go to Memorial Stadium, which was on the other side of town.

"Everybody went, you wouldn't miss it for the world," said Scott Redd, who hung out with Sandra at Olympic High.

Busing students from other neighborhoods and schools, areas that had been primarily black, did serve to beef up the football team and give it a good mix of athletic talent. "The football team went from 2A level to 4A because a lot of kids came over from South Mecklenburg. We had a fairly decent football team before, but all of a sudden it was really great. That year we went on to the state championship; it was instant football glory," said Jimmy Niell, who played slotback on the Trojan team.

Joe White, who coached at Olympic for sixteen years, knew he had a pretty good team. "We went to the state finals and had the best record that year, one that still stands," he said, beaming. He was proud of his players and always tried to encourage them, especially the ones he knew were struggling financially. When the Trojans would have a big win, he and his wife would invite everyone over to their house to celebrate; the coach knew the kids didn't have the money to go out, and a lot of them couldn't afford cars.

"We started a tradition. After a game, when we wanted to unwind, we would have the team over to our house and fix peanut butter [sandwiches] and baloney sandwiches and my wife would make a pound cake.

"And where the boys would go, the girls would follow," he added.

By early 1970s standards, the students were from all-American, God-fearing families who raised their children to attend Sunday school and church every week and to say the blessing before meals.

Less than that in Charlotte, North Carolina, would have

been considered a disgrace, since the city, which had a mix of 58 percent white, 33 percent black, was in the heart of the conservative Bible Belt.

With 700 places to worship, Charlotte was dubbed "The City of Churches." It was home to evangelist Billy Graham and eventually fertile ground for the evangelical PTL—Praise The Lord—television ministry headed by the infamous Jim and Tammy Faye Bakker.

In the late 1980s PTL built a 120-acre Christian complex in Fort Mill, South Carolina, just minutes from Charlotte, called Heritage USA. The retreat and conference center drew 100,000 people a year until Jim Bakker became involved in a sex scandal with his secretary Jessica Hahn.

An investigation eventually led to Bakker's imprisonment for mail and wire fraud. In the end he was accused of bilking PTL supporters out of more than 750 million dollars. It was a major embarrassment, because God and country were at the forefront of the community. The Lord's Prayer was recited before every assembly, and the American flag was saluted at all of the athletic events.

ROTC was becoming more popular as the boys began to pay attention to the Vietnam War, which was on the news every night. With discussions of the draft in the headlines, the students knew they would be called into military service if they weren't going on to college after graduation—and many had no hope of a college education.

"None of the guys wanted to go to Vietnam," said Ronnie Stack, who knew Sandra and Sally in high school. "Nixon was President then and the South was predominantly Democrat. That was the old South, this is a new world," he said. Then, the entire population of Charlotte was around 150,000. "We were a small, tight-knit group. We all knew each other. The athletes especially knew everyone in town."

The 1970s were considered the "new birth of Charlotte," but it was undergoing some horrendous contractions to be reborn, with almost daily race riots because of forced busing.

"That was a scary time," recalls one student.

"I was raised in a family where race didn't matter, but it was really stressful for some of the kids. We had never gone to school with blacks before," explained Pam Sargent, Sally's best friend in high school.

"The whole apple cart was upset, we were all just trying to get to know each other, since people were being bused to Olympic," Stark added. "There were definitely concerns and racial strife," added former Coach White. At one point, he says, the doors had to be taken off of all the restrooms at the school. "Otherwise there was a good chance someone would get jumped in the bathroom."

Jimmy Niell recalls that Charlotte and Olympic High were on the national news every night because of the racial tension. "Sometimes it would be two hundred versus two hundred in the mall area in the middle of the school. Almost every day a fight would escalate into cars and school buses being turned over. They [the school administration] didn't want to have a police presence at the school to enforce busing, but the police ended up coming every day to get things settled back down," Niell recalled. "You never knew when a shove in the hall would lead to a full-scale riot."

Still, there were plenty of good times to be had in the 70s, when life was far less complicated. Television programs like *The Andy Griffith Show* depicted the simple life of Mayberry, which was actually filmed in and modeled after Mount Airy, a small North Carolina town. Fonzie's life on *Happy Days* didn't seem to be a big stretch of the imagination.

"Those were the best years of my life," says Robbie

Byrum, a close friend of Sandra's throughout high school who went on to have several successful businesses.

In fact, southwest Charlotte, where Olympic High was built, was still farmland. There were only a handful of houses nearby, families who were farming the land as their ancestors had done before them.

"I had several kids that would leave football practice and go home to milk cows or work on the tractor," the coach recalled. Kids from Olympic, especially the athletes, had a hard time living down the "hick" image because the area was still rural country.

"We lived way in the country. I remember one time me and Robbie took the hay wagon to school," said Jimmy Niell.

Like most 15- and 16-year-olds, the most pressing issue on their minds was what was going on in their world: the cute new girl or boy in their class and who won the Friday night football or basketball game.

"American Pie" was a hit on the record charts. Although the Beatles had disbanded, they were still popular, especially the music of John Lennon and Paul McCartney. Radio DJs played a stream of Bee Gees, Bob Dylan and Crosby, Stills, Nash & Young hits, and although it was before the psychedelic music phase really hit the country, Pink Floyd was beginning to attract attention.

Early on in high school, everyone hung out together. They would all end up at the same pizza place after a game or run into each other at the same parties, always as a group.

"We might recognize someone and talk to them at a party, but we didn't necessarily go there together," explained Mark Perry. "We were just having innocent fun."

Coach White described the students as "good kids." "I don't really remember any troublemakers; they were absolutely good citizens."

As for the popular clique, Robbie Byrum said, "We had a little clan." They were "the in crowd," the people who were considered "cool," "downtown" or high class, says Ronnie Stack.

They were clean-cut girls who wore fashionable short skirts, although not too short, shirtwaist dresses and culottes. Most of them had their hair long and straight or loosely curled. Boys were just beginning to wear T-shirts and jeans—the older the better—or cords with their shirttails hanging out and Wallabees, the predecessor to Hush Puppies. Most of the boys had short hair; some let it grow a little over the ear like the early Beatles, but if they were athletes, that could get them in trouble.

"Some of the football players would show up with long hair sticking out of their helmets, but that just wasn't acceptable," recalled White, who says he wouldn't be as strict about hair length today.

The cheerleading squad consisted of junior and senior girls whose selection was considered a badge of honor. There were also letter girls, a majorette and the flag corps, the Trojanettes, which was part of Larry Wells' incredible band, the Marching Trojans. "The band was so popular, sometimes I think people just came to the games to see it," said Coach White.

Classmates say the school had several distinct groups: jocks (or preppies), hippies, Jesus freaks, free spirits and blacks. Olympic High's quasi-hippies were easy to spot—girls with unkempt flowing hair, with beads, peasant blouses and boots, and anything with fringe; the boys tried to make a statement with long hair (sometimes worn in a ponytail), tie-dyed T-shirts and Dingo boots. The hippies were different from "free spirits," recalled self-professed hippie Ronnie Stack, who admits he would skip school to hang out at the river. Sally was a free spirit, but could fit in with any of the groups—preppies, Jesus freaks, or hippies—he claimed.

"The free spirits didn't feel they had to fit into any mold. She liked to hang out and have a beer with the boys on Friday night after the game. She didn't put as much focus on where a guy fit into society, and she definitely didn't seek out athletes."

They all did the usual things; after football and basketball games they would hit Pizza Hut or Pizza Inn. Sometimes they had hamburgers at McDonald's on South Boulevard or go to a movie. Once in a while they would have a beer and get a slight buzz, but for the most part there didn't seem to be any heavy drinking or drugs in their group. Or as Ronnie Stack put it, "They were 'closet partyers'; they never wanted anyone to know they were partying like everyone else."

Looking back, Stack says it was easy to see where the chips would fall class-wise. "The in crowd turned out to be Republicans, always interested in the almighty dollar. A lot of the cheerleaders would only date boys who were going to college and were likely to make good money." He believed Sandra fell into that category.

The kids in the "outer circle," who had something on their minds other than making lots of money, turned out to be the Democrats. Sally, he said, is a Democrat. "She liked all the boys, she didn't only date the up-and-comers."

In high school, none of them were troublemakers. "Sometimes I would get a whiff of pot in the stairwell, but it wasn't widespread," recalled White. "My wife and I chaperoned every dance they had at Olympic High, and sometimes we would have to ask someone to leave because they had been drinking, but that was the exception to the rule. I would just have my coaching staff at the dance, and there usually wouldn't be any trouble."

Mark Perry, who was a member of the student council, was friendly with everyone at school, black and white, jocks and hippies. He met Sandra and Sally in junior high. He considered himself a close friend of Sandra's; Sally was more like an acquaintance, he said, someone he would stop and talk to in the hall at school or when he saw her at a party. He knew Sandra much better and would often hang out with her and her best friend Kay White; on the weekend the three of them would go out together to eat or catch a movie. They would also go down to the lake where Mark's family kept a boat.

"When Sandra and Kay were together, it was something," he added. "They were a ball of energy when they got together."

Robbie Byrum used to be big buddies with Sandra until he started dating Joy in the 10th grade, the girl who became the most important female in his life. They married after school and are still together. "Sandra was a big cut-up, you always had fun with her," he recalled.

Sandra Baker was the all-American girl with long blonde hair, huge brown eyes and a smile that would instantly light up a room. She was always upbeat and had a positive attitude about everything.

"She was on top of the world no matter what," said a classmate.

Sandra was born May 28, 1955, the youngest of two girls whose parents, Roy and Betty Baker, were middle class, but seemed to be financially comfortable. Her father had been a Navy career man, and ran a tight ship. Her mother Betty was a homemaker who doted on her family, which was often the case in that era.

Sandra's pretty older sister Debbie, who had attended Olympic High two years before, had been a popular cheerleader. Sandra was also a cheerleader, in junior high and then as part of the Trojan cheerleader squad for three years. In her junior and senior years at Olympic, she was the team captain. Everyone knew who she was. She was smart, vivacious and an outstanding leader.

Rusty Alexander, who dated Sandra for a few months during the 9th and 10th grades said, "She was always involved in a lot of things in high school, she always had a rah-rah spirit."

The 1972 yearbook indicates that she was involved in several extracurricular activities, including the pep club and student council.

She always thought she would be a teacher, but even more important, she dreamed of having a family one day.

"She was always very focused and disciplined. She was always the one to go above and beyond, like getting all the signs out for a pep rally. She was always a take-charge person," Mark Perry said.

Cheerleaders were considered the cream of the crop, the prize. Sandra, in particular, was incredibly popular and a large part of Olympic High's landscape.

Thirty years after high school, Mark Perry was devastated when he heard that Sandra had died. "I cried when I heard about her death. She had so much to offer, so much to give."

Scott Redd, whose sister Julie had been one of Sandra's best friends in high school, was shaken to the core.

Like so many, he had admired her from afar. "Sure, I wanted to date her," he says more than thirty years later, but he had to get used to just being his sister's "little brother."

Shortly after Sandra's separation from John, Scott and Sandra began running into each other at the upscale Palm restaurant; he always introduced her to the people he knew, and he and his girlfriend invited her to join them at several parties.

Unfortunately they hadn't been in touch for a few months, since the beginning of 2001.

He was at the beach on April 10 when Julie called to tell him that Sandra was dead.

"I couldn't believe it. It was heartbreaking," he said.

"I was in shock when she died. How could this happen to such a beautiful girl? She didn't need to have plastic surgery, I don't even know why she would have it done," he says, still grappling with the tragedy years later.

But it was all certainly reason to get in touch with each other again.

Joye Byrum, who married high school sweetheart Robbie Byrum, was a fellow cheerleader at Olympic High School and Sandra's friend. She told *The Charlotte Observer* that Sandra was always a real go-getter. "She could be headstrong if she wanted something."

But Joye wouldn't respond to any other questions from local or national media about her good friend, saying, "I really don't know anything."

High school boyfriend and later husband John Joyner said Sandra excelled at everything she ever did. "She was always perfect; she was the perfect student and the perfect cheerleader. She was perfect in everything she did. And most of all, she was always really pretty, inside and out."

Schoolmate Sally Jordan was younger and graduated a year after Sandra. She was adorable, with shoulder-length blonde hair and beautiful blue eyes.

Sally had been a cheerleader in junior high; some say she tried out for cheerleading in high school but didn't make the squad. She played in the Olympic High band, the Marching Trojans, was the head of the flag corps and an alternate letter girl, which drew her into the popular clique of cheerleaders and athletes.

She didn't appear to be as involved in school activities

as Sandra. The Trojan yearbook makes no mention of her participation in any clubs. In fact, she is not listed in the 1973 Olympic High yearbook at all, and some thought maybe she left school for a while.

"I hated high school. I just wanted to graduate and move to some place like New York. I thought Charlotte was nothing more than a big truck stop," she explained.

Friends say Sally had a great sense of humor and loved to have fun, but she could be serious and moody at times. She clearly wasn't as extroverted as Sandra.

"On a scale, I would say she was happy about seventy to seventy-five percent of the time," said one classmate.

But Dennis Poston, who dated Sally in high school, said, "She wasn't any [moodier] than any other girl."

Scott Redd recalled that she was really smart. But he also recalls that she was not in "the in crowd."

Scott hung out with Sally in junior high when they had some classes together. In fact, he took her to the junior high school prom at the end of the 9th grade.

"We weren't boyfriend and girlfriend; I just needed someone to take, and I had heard she didn't have a date," he explained.

After junior high, he says, they didn't see each other as often. "In high school we ran with different crowds. Sally was popular, she just ran with a different group than I did," he said referring to the fact that he was part of "the in crowd." Sally, he said, "was a little more spirited," meaning she was part of the group that didn't feel the need to conform to what was "in."

An only child, Sally was born February 23, 1956, in Charlotte, to loving parents who were described as good people who were very protective of her.

"When I was born my dad was a traveling salesman, but my mother put a stop to that right away," Sally said with a laugh. Her father was named Clinton LeGette by his mother, who lived in rural South Carolina, but he disliked the name Clinton so much that he had everyone call him LeGette, she explained. During her early school days, Sally's father worked for Sears, Roebuck, but when she was in high school he started his own business, Jordan Carpet Company. Her father had a heart attack when she was 17 years old and decided that doing handyman-type services—stain and repair work—would be less stressful. Though it turned out to be something he really enjoyed, it just wasn't as lucrative.

A high school friend remembered the Jordans moving around a lot. He referred to them as "a moving target," speculating that it was so her father could find work. The family wasn't as well off as the Bakers, but Sally's parents always provided a loving home with a good moral foundation based on a strong religious faith.

"Her parents were very protective and kept close reins on her," said Dennis Poston, who dated Sally in the 9th and 10th grades. "She had a nice family. They were very religious, so that was a major part of her life. And she was really close to them, since she was the only child."

As much as everyone liked both girls, they seemed to consider Sandra the grand prize.

"Everybody adored her," said Mark. "She was always going to be on top of the world no matter what."

Everyone said Sandra could have her pick of boys, except that her parents didn't let her date very much at the beginning of high school, a classmate said.

When Sandra met John Joyner, a good-looking athlete on the school wrestling team during her junior year, it wasn't long before they were going steady.

To many it seemed natural, since he was a wrestler and she was a cheerleader. He was handsome and smart, she was beautiful and vivacious. They were the Ken and Barbie of Olympic High School.

John was well-liked, too. He was a good person, but classmates didn't seem to know him as well as Sandra, because he was a year ahead of her and most of her friends. No one remembered him dating anyone steadily in high school until he met Sandra.

"We were really good friends, but he could be kind of shy until you got to know him," explained Jimmy Niell, who was on the wrestling team with John.

The wrestling team was close-knit. John was a year ahead of Jimmy, but they wrestled the same weight class, 145 pounds.

"When I was a sophomore, we would have sophomore/junior/senior wrestle-offs to see who would get to wrestle the next two matches. I could beat John, John could beat the senior, but the senior could beat me," he recalled.

Back then John's family owned and ran Joyner's Restaurant, a landmark eatery at Lake Wylie Marina near the Buster Boyd Bridge on the South Carolina state line.

"It was always popular," Jimmy said.

John's parents split when he was in high school. His mother stayed at Lake Wylie and ran the restaurant. John's brother Mike also ran it for a while, until she sold it.

"I always thought John was a really nice guy. We got along real well. Obviously he must have been real smart, he's always done well for himself," said Jimmy.

John was a senior at Olympic High, Sandra a junior when the relationship really began to get serious.

Sally was also well-liked and popular, especially with the boys, but she wasn't as bubbly as Sandra, according to friends. Her wicked sense of humor was remembered by everyone; it was her trademark.

"She was really cute and a lot of fun to be with. She loved to have a good time," said Dennis Poston, who continued to see Sally on and off for a couple of years after high school.

"She wasn't shy, she was just quieter," said Scott Redd. "And I do remember her being really smart."

Pam Sargent, who was Sally's best friend in junior high and high school, recalled Sally getting along well with everyone. "We would spend the night at each other's house and do all the things girls do together, like go to slumber parties. And we were always shopping."

Pam has fond memories of a group of girls going to the beach together, and staying at Cherry Grove near Myrtle Beach, South Carolina. Days were spent on the beach, and early evenings they would head to the Pavilion to ride the famous roller coaster and check out the T-shirt shops and boys on the main drag.

By the time the girls got to junior high, they were just beginning to wear pants to school, she recalled. They had to watch their hemlines and would get in trouble if their skirts were too short.

"Until the seventh grade we couldn't wear pants at all. Our home economics teacher would make us stand on the table and measure our skirts to make sure they weren't too short," she explained. "But as soon as we left class we would just roll the waistband over to make the skirts shorter."

In a particularly nostalgic moment, Pam also recalls Sally's bedroom, where she would have sleepovers and the girls would spend hours talking. "I still remember she had those hippie beads in her room. Now my daughter has some just like the ones hanging in Sally's room," she said.

Classmates described Sally as being pretty easy-going; neither Pam nor Dennis ever knew her to be really mad at anyone.

"Oh, the girls all got into spats, they would get sideways with each other, that's all," Pam recalled. "I never knew her to be mad at anyone, she certainly wouldn't fight over anybody."

Pam takes issue with the fact that Sandra has been portrayed as the more popular of the girls, especially the speculation that Sally might have been jealous of Sandra. Pam said it was Sally who was the real hit with the boys.

"She always had a boyfriend. Sandra's parents didn't let her date much before John. It certainly wasn't a case of Sally being jealous, she always had boys hanging around her," she added.

Several of her male classmates mentioned that Sally was considered somewhat promiscuous.

"She certainly wasn't sweet and innocent," said one classmate. Another described her as "loose."

But that may have been simply because Sally would go out with a group of boys after a game on Friday for a beer, or because she dated a lot of boys, rather than going steady. She would see someone for a couple of months, then move on to the next guy, explained one of her classmates.

In contrast, Sandra tended to "go steady" for a period of time with the people she dated.

When Pam would stay over at Sally's house, she didn't often see Sally's father, LeGette, who had health problems over the years and died in January 2006. She said he was hardly ever around. All she remembered about Sally's mother Alice was that she had short blonde hair and wore glasses.

But Dennis remembers running into Sally's father quite a bit. He really liked LeGette, who once gave him a harmonica.

"He was bald, about five feet nine inches, a heavy-set man. He was always on a diet, he never ate anything but steak," he said.

The last couple of years in high school, all the kids who

ran around together as a group began to break off into
smaller cliques and started to date. They would go out to
eat, see a movie, or catch up with friends. They often
double-dated with others in the group. If they were dating
steadily, the girl would wear the boy's class ring; sometimes it dangled from a chain around her neck.

It was a socially conservative time. "A lot of times we
would go to church with our girlfriends," explained Mark
Perry. Sex was something that was generally reserved for
marriage, or at least until you were in a steady relationship, he added.

It was not unusual when a couple would break up that
both parties might end up dating someone else in the
same group, or a friend of a friend. No one thought anything about it when Jimmy Niell, who was said to have
been hanging out with Sally for a short time, began dating
Sandra, long before she met John.

"Yeah, I remember they were hanging out for a while.
Then he starting dating Sandra after that," Mark Perry recalled.

Jimmy Niell was the school "chick magnet." He was
handsome, with lots of charisma. He played sideback on
the Trojan football team and was on the star wrestling
team that won the district championship several years and
barely missed out on the state championship.

While he was adorable, classmates say it was his personality that made him so popular. "He was a cut-up, he
ran around with a whole group of kids that were funny.
He wasn't a ladies' man, he just always had a good time,
he was a character," said Scott Redd.

Most of Sandra and Sally's classmates were not aware
of any hard feelings between the girls; they were all part of
the same large group, and would often end up at the same
events.

"I never thought Sally and Sandy [Sandra] knew each

other that well. I certainly never saw any friction between them," Mark adds.

It wasn't until years after Sandra's death that a confidential source told *The Charlotte Observer* and law enforcement that Sandra and Sally, who had merely been acquaintances, not friends, "never got along, a grudge had been brewing for years," supposedly over the boyfriend Sally was said to have believed that Sandra took away from her. To this day no one knows the identity of the informant, but the allegation fueled the fire into murder charges. In particular the newspaper mentioned that in 1999, when Sandra came to Dr. Tucker for a procedure on one of her eyes, Sally had pointed Sandra out to a coworker saying that Sandra was "the one who had stolen my boyfriend in high school."

Pam Sargent said that doesn't sound at all likely. "I'm not even sure that particular boy—Jimmy Niell—ever knew anyone had a crush on him," she said flatly.

Pam moved to another high school in her junior year and lost touch with Sally. They haven't spoken since those sleepover days at Olympic High School.

In one of the newspaper articles, Joye Byrum, who was the closest to Sandra, told an *Observer* reporter that she wasn't even aware that the two girls knew each other, except that they would coincidentally end up at the same event.

"There was never any mention of Sally, or of any problem with her," Joye said.

John Joyner, who saw Sandra every day in high school, also said that he wasn't aware that Sandra and Sally knew each other. He had never heard Sandra mention her name or say anything about the girls not getting along.

"Back then I heard through the grapevine that they had some trouble over a boy, or Sandra being more popular, but I don't know any details," said Ronnie Stack, who knew both girls. "When I heard about Sandra's death, I couldn't believe I had known one of the women really well and the other one was accused of murdering her," he added.

Sandra Baker's untimely death—under such mysterious circumstances—stunned her former classmates and became a double whammy when they learned that another classmate, Sally Jordan, had been the nurse who had assisted in her surgery and was thought to have given her the fatal dose of pain medication.

And that was years before Sally would be accused of murdering Sandra.

While many others have said they were not aware of any feud between the girls, some in the group did observe that Sally may have been overshadowed by Sandra's presence, that she may have considered herself second best, walking in Sandra's shadow. That, of course, could have an impact on anyone's ego.

"Anybody who thought they could compete with Sandra was in for a surprise, because she had it all," said Mark Perry.

"She did everything well, that's one reason she was so popular," explained John. "She was liked by everybody, she just never had an enemy."

Or did she?

THREE

Late Seventies: Adulthood

By the time they were ready to graduate from high school, both Sandra and Sally had mapped out plans for their lives as adults.

Sandra and John had been dating since they met toward the end of high school. They really hadn't dated anyone else seriously, and they were planning to make a life together. After high school they both attended Western Carolina University near Asheville, where John studied business and Sandra earned a degree in physical education.

On June 22, 1979, after graduating from college, *the perfect couple said their vows* in a lovely wedding at the Belk Chapel in historical Myers Park with several hundred family members and friends looking on. The chapel, which was donated to Queens College by William Henry Belk's heirs, is still a popular wedding location because of its warm atmosphere and historic architecture.

Sandra was a radiant bride in a traditional long white wedding dress with lace and an elegant veil. She had six bridesmaids and John had six attendants. The ceremony was performed by the minister of Sandra's tiny nondenominational church off Woodlawn Road.

"I seem to remember the pastor had a slight Scottish

accent," said John, who attended a Greek Orthodox Church, but said he'd deferred to Sandra—as was usually the case, he admitted—to decide who would perform the ceremony.

A reception followed in an older building next to the Belk Chapel, that had fine furnishings and was often rented out for receptions and meetings. John had discovered the building when he was in high school. "When I went to Myers Park High School, I found it when we would go to the Queens College campus for different events. I suggested it when Sandra and I were planning the wedding," he said. "We only paid a couple of hundred dollars for it."

After college John went to work as an accountant for Dickerson Group, Inc., a mining and road-paving company in Monroe, North Carolina, that specializes in highway, street and bridge construction. He was dedicated to his work, and was often the first to arrive in the office in the morning and the last to leave at night.

Sandra taught 7th and 8th grade health and physical education in the Charlotte-Mecklenburg school system and coached volleyball. She was a wonderful teacher who was loved by all the kids.

In 1984, five years after she and John married, Sandra left her career behind when their first son John Grayson was born. After that, Sandra followed in her mother's footsteps, devoting all of her time to being a homemaker and mother, caring for their two sons and tending to their lovely two-story traditional brick home with a perfectly manicured lawn. In 1986 their second son, Philip Edward, was born.

"She loved being a mother, and there wasn't a better one. She and the kids were joined at the hip, they were always very close," John recalled.

John, who was wound pretty tightly, was driven to succeed in his career. He worked long hours and often traveled, leaving Sandra to take up the slack, shuttling the boys to and from school, athletic events and community activities. Both boys were good students who played intramural sports, T-ball, track and basketball. Sandra was always there to cheer them on, a devoted team mother who took pride in her sons' accomplishments.

The Joyners were homebodies. Everything they did revolved around the boys, whom they adored. They made sure they all had dinner together every night, and they were all in bed by 10:30 p.m. When they did eat out at a restaurant, which was not very often, it was all four of them. Evenings and weekends were spent helping the kids with homework.

"That was our life," says John.

In retrospect, he realized that he and Sandra should have carved out some time just for the two of them. By the time John had worked his way up from accountant to chief financial officer and then president and owner of the company, the boys were teens establishing their own lives, and John and Sandra had drifted apart.

In 1999 the couple separated. John has suggested that he and Sandra grew apart because he was in the business world and Sandra wasn't, saying they were on different wavelengths. But some have suggested that their split occurred because he became involved with someone else.

John remained in the house at 3925 Huntcliff Drive in south Charlotte, where they had lived as a family, and Sandra moved to Post Park at Phillips Place, a nearby community of upscale apartments, high-end retail shops and restaurants like The Palm and Dean & DeLuca. The boys, who were in high school, divided their time between their parents, depending on their school and sports schedules. For Grayson, as everyone called him, and Philip's sake, their parents were working hard to be as amicable as possible to hold the family together as best they could.

At one of the Olympic High School Career Days, Sally had stopped by the University of North Carolina at Charlotte booth to inquire about a career as an anesthesiologist. Her first step, she was told, was to get a nursing degree.

After graduating from high school she began the process of putting herself through college to become a certified nurse anesthetist. She entered a four-year nursing program at Central Piedmont Community College in Charlotte, earning a registered nurse's license in 1982. For eight years she worked two days a week at Presbyterian Hospital in the recovery room, and three days a week at Presbyterian Orthopaedic Hospital. In 1996 she returned to school to get her nurse anesthetist's certification at Carolinas Medical Center.

During her time at Presbyterian Hospital she had worked with several different plastic surgeons, including Dr. Peter Tucker. When Dr. Tucker left the hospital to join practice with Dr. Thomas Giblin and Dr. William Laird, Sally went with him. Two years later, when Dr. Tucker decided to open the Center for Cosmetic and Plastic Surgery clinic, she joined him as his contract nurse anesthetist.

Most of Sally's friends had married much earlier. She had been to her share of showers and weddings, and had outfitted babies for several of her friends by the time she met Jim Hill.

She was 26 when she married Jim, who had a good job with United Parcel Service.

"He was one of the first men I had dated that hadn't been married before, which was important to me," she explained. "And he liked cats."

He was good with money; he had his own condo and a

nice car. She remembered him calling to tell her he had a new stereo, which turned out to be in his new BMW.

Between them they were making good money.

"When we married, we were making the same thing, but over the years his salary stayed the same and mine tripled."

The couple bought a beautiful house with some land on the outskirts of Charlotte, hoping they would have a family. But they never did.

"I know it was a disappointment that they never had children, I know they wanted them," explained Anita Hill, Sally's mother-in-law.

"They had cats instead," she added.

Initially Sally and Jim seemed to share the same interests. They both liked camping and buying old cars and fixing them up.

"Well, he would fix them up, I would help finance them," Sally explained.

But in 1995, when Sally was "born again" in a religious sense, and wanted to live her faith on a daily basis, the couple began to grow apart.

"I was saved again, but he didn't want any part of it. He didn't like the music, he wouldn't go to church with me, he didn't even want to go to parties we had at church," she explained.

Neither seemed to be happy in the marriage. It was as if they were just going through the motions as they approached their twentieth wedding anniversary.

"They are both really nice people, they just didn't have much in common," said Anita Hill. Her only explanation for them growing apart was, "She's a Democrat and he's a Republican."

In spite of the difficult times between Sally and Jim, his mother seemed to genuinely like Sally. "We never had a bad word in the twenty years they were married," she bragged.

Everyone who knew Sally described her the same way.

"She is jolly, she loves to laugh. She's a really fun person," said close friend Patty Campbell, a circulating nurse who worked with Sally at Dr. Tucker's office until 1999.

Sally's wit and her kindness were traits everyone seemed to notice.

"She's nice and really nurturing. She's just a really kind and sincere person," said John G. Golding, the attorney who represented Sally in the malpractice suit filed by John Joyner after Sandra's death.

"When Sally is hurt, she's devastated, and when she's happy, it shows. She's a breath of fresh air," said a longtime friend who is a professional hairdresser and cuts Sally's hair. "She's always thinking of others, and she's the first one to encourage them. I know Sally's heart. She has never even thought of hurting someone, much less killing them."

But the Sally Hill who was eventually brought before the North Carolina Board of Nursing in 2003 and was found to have multiple violations of the Nursing Practice Act at the time of Sandra's death seemed to be a very different person from the one family and friends had described.

FOUR

Sandra's Perfect Life

Life had turned out as planned for Sandra, it seemed—until the last couple of years before her death.

Like so many couples who marry young, John and Sandra had drifted apart by the time they had been married for eighteen years. John blamed the fact that they were both approaching mid-life and neither of them had really ever dated anyone else before they married. "When two people have known each other for twenty-five years and they're hitting a mid-life crisis, the pressure of the American lifestyle just breaks them down," he explained. "We both needed to get out and find out what we wanted to do."

Still, in John's opinion, during the two-year separation, they had both grown a lot; he had seen Sandra become more independent in those last years. He had always believed they would get back together some day.

"She had to do a lot on her own for the first time," said John. "She had never had to be independent before. We had always been together. We needed time away. I think we both grew up in those years that we were separated."

For years Sandra had what appeared to be the perfect life. She certainly never dreamed that their marriage wouldn't survive. She had always been a homebody caring for her family. She had never had to fend for herself, make a salary or balance a budget; she had never even lived alone before. The separation shook her to the core, and probably for the first time in her life, her self-esteem was suffering.

Occasionally high school classmates would run into Sandra and John around town. "She always looked the same, and seemed just as friendly," recalled Scott Redd.

John Joyner was a little harder to read in their brief meetings.

"He was hard to describe. He was kind of quiet. He never had much to say—it was always as if he didn't have time to talk to you," Scott said. "I don't think he was the easiest person to get along with."

Sandra's life was completely different now. She was within walking distance of fine restaurants, a wine bar and The Palm, where "the beautiful people" gathered for drinks after work every day.

"I give her credit, she was a strong-willed lady," John said of her starting a new life. "She was always strong, very decisive; I was the one that would mealy-mouth around."

Initially Sandra was struggling to adjust to her new life, which was not one of her choosing. She was trying to get back in the job market, but other than teaching for a few years, her only other job experience had been working part-time in human resources with her sister at Marshall Air Systems. She had never really been out there in the business world on her own, and she found the prospects daunting.

"There's a toughness that comes with working out in the world," said John. "She was used to being a team mother; she kept the house; it was the American way."

When the couple first separated, Sandra had trouble coping, as any woman would in her situation. John said she was depressed; some days she couldn't even get out of bed. He said she had started taking antidepressants to lift her spirits and help her cope.

But to most people it looked like Sandra was still living the good life. She was driving a new white Mercedes Coupe convertible and she lived at Post Park Apartment Homes, which range in price from $750 a month for a one-bedroom to $3,000 a month for a three-bedroom apartment. All the bills were paid by John.

The luxurious complex was built around a man-made lake. There were courtyards with fountains, and a pool and fitness center. It was within walking distance of high-end shopping, fine restaurants, a movie theater and a hair salon.

Post Park attracted a nice group of professionals who often met for monthly socials arranged by the apartment management. After a while Sandra made some single girl friends and they would go out together to nearby bars and restaurants for dinner and drinks. John says he and Sandra had discussed the prospects of her dating, which after eighteen years of marriage, was even more daunting than the job market. "Dating is hard; it's deep and it's cold out there," he said. "I could sympathize with her."

Sandra hadn't been single since she was in high school; it was certainly a different experience in 2000. She was aware that she was competing with much younger women in the job market as well as in the singles scene.

"Sandra was always interested in the dollar. She was from a blue-collar family like the rest of us, but she always wanted to be around money," recalled Ronnie Stack.

She had a good life with John, who ran with the city's movers and shakers and had even had a couple of fund-raisers for Charlotte Mayor Pat McCrory, who is running for governor of North Carolina.

"She had always been married," said Stack. "After they separated, she wanted to be in the in crowd with the

movers and shakers. She wanted to fit in, and she was
too old. She was hanging out with the people I call 'the
Phillips Place/Palm people'—who wanted to be with
young women."

In her desire to be in the in crowd, she had inadvertently hooked up with a couple of big-time gamblers, an
acquaintance says. "In high school she seemed to only go
out with the boys she thought were going somewhere [fi-
nancially]. Apparently she was still chasing the money,"
Stack added.

Sandra seemed to take it especially hard when she
didn't get a job that she had really wanted with US Airways. She was convinced it was because they wanted
someone younger. It was then she decided a little work on
her face would give her a more "rested" look; it would
erase the stress of the last couple of years, soften the lines
and dark shadows that she had begun to notice.

"I didn't oppose it. She was going to have the same
doctor and nurse she had before when she had a procedure done on one of her eyes," John explained. Sandra
had always had one eye that was larger than the other, one
that drooped, he said. The average person would never
have noticed it, but he said she had talked about it ever
since he had known her.

John had taken her to the Center for Cosmetic and
Plastic Surgery appointment two years earlier for the surgery on her eye. He had waited for her to come out from
under the anesthesia and been there to help her through the
healing. "We just sat in the recovery room until she got
over the anesthetic and then we went home. I took care of
her for about a week, she just stayed indoors and took it
easy. She didn't have any problems," he recalled.

Even more important, she was happy with the results.
"I don't think anyone even knew she had the procedure
done, but she felt better about it," John explained.

For Sandra, the surgery in 2001 was different from the first. She was trying to reinvent herself. She had a lot of new stresses living on her own. She was out on the town several times a week with friends at The Palm and other hot spots. She didn't really want to change her looks, she just wanted to look like herself when she was younger. If a mini-facelift and laser resurfacing would help her feel better about herself, John, who was footing the bill, saw no harm in it.

"In some ways her natural good looks may have made her mid-life crisis even more difficult," he mused. "If you grow up with a lot of good looks, it's hard to see them fade as you get older." But most people were simply puzzled.

"She was gorgeous, she didn't need to have any surgery, she could have anybody she wanted," said Scott Redd.

The night before her surgery, Sandra went over to the house where she had lived for so many years to visit with the boys and John. Although the couple was legally separated, they were making every effort to get along for the boys' sake.

It was a cool spring evening, so the family sat on the front porch, John and Sandra in the large rocking chairs, Grayson and Philip on the front steps. They talked about the boys' sports activities, how the teams were doing and what was happening at school. They laughed together like old times.

John had offered to take Sandra to her appointment the next morning, but she told him that her mother and sister were taking her.

"So I just said OK and wished her luck," he recalled.

John was under the impression that Sandra's family was taking her to her appointment that morning. He was later surprised to learn that she had taken a cab. Quite possibly a family member was picking her up after the procedure.

The boys had wanted to go home with Sandra that last

night, but their parents decided it would be better for them to stay with John, since they had school the next day. So around 10 p.m. Sandra hugged John and the boys, who both towered over her, and headed for her apartment.

"I'm so glad she came by that night; it was so good for all of us," John recalled.

She had assured them that everything would be fine. It would be just like it was when she'd had the earlier procedure. It was at the same place, with the same doctor and the same nurse.

There was nothing to be concerned about.

FIVE

Sally's Working Life

Sally Jordan had often talked about being a nurse anesthetist, so in 1974, after graduating from Olympic High, she became a registered nurse, which was the first step toward her chosen career.

She was putting herself through school because her parents couldn't afford the tuition. She was a good student at Central Piedmont Community College where she received an associate's degree in nursing. Then she went on to Carolinas Medical Center for her anethetist's certification.

"Out of a class of eighty, only twenty made it," she said proudly.

People who knew her said Sally had always seemed to be a natural caregiver, a hallmark for being a good nurse.

After getting her nursing license in 1977, Sally began working at Presbyterian Hospital in Charlotte and later moved to the Presbyterian Orthopaedic Hospital. All told, she worked in the hospital system for over ten years.

"Sally was a wonderful anesthetist," said Sandy Stumpf, who worked with Sally at the hospital. "She was always a joy to be around."

It was in nursing school that Sally met Jim Hill, a local boy, one of four sons in the Hill family, who seemed to be a perfect complement to her. They were both 26. He had a good job with United Parcel Service, his own condo and a nice car. They seemed to want the same things, including a family.

On September 4, 1982, the couple was married at the First Baptist Church of Charlotte. Her three attendants—a cousin, her best friend and a nurse she worked with—were in the wedding party wearing beautiful long pink gowns. Jim had three groomsmen by his side.

"It was the typical Baptist wedding," as Sally described it.

Sally's father LeGette proudly escorted the bride, who was wearing a simple white gown without a lot of adornment, down the aisle.

Sally was conscious of the fact that her family couldn't afford a lavish wedding.

"Even in 1982 you could end up having to pay four hundred dollars for a wedding dress," she said. "I found the perfect dress for seventy-five dollars and got a hat for seventy-five dollars."

Sally told everyone she didn't want to have a wedding reception because she didn't want her parents to have to foot the expense. But a church member made a sour cream wedding cake, another decorated the church basement and they had a lovely reception for family and friends.

"I always thought that showed how much they thought of my family to help them out like that," Sally proudly recounted.

To this day she still vividly remembers that sour cream wedding cake.

"I wasn't aware how wonderful it was that day, because there was so much going on, but a year later we ate the top layer that we had kept in the freezer. That's when I realized how really delicious it was."

Only one high school classmate recalled running into

Sally after graduating from Olympic High. He saw her at the popular restaurant Johnny Dollars, then later at the high school reunion, where he commented on her weight gain.

Still, she had a promising career. By then Dr. Tucker was a well-known and respected plastic surgeon with a loyal patient base. Sally worked side by side with him as his contract anesthetist, and they performed thousands of surgeries together.

According to the Center for Cosmetic and Plastic Surgery website ituck.net Dr. Tucker has been performing plastic surgery in Charlotte for over a decade, specializing in breast enlargement, facelifts and other plastic surgery, with extremely satisfied patients.

"We believe a better informed individual makes a better patient," touts a tagline that is also used in print ads that run in high-end lifestyle magazines. "Dr. Tucker believes each and every one of his patients deserve the very best. He truly wants to help each patient be the very best they can be. Using cosmetic surgery and nonsurgical procedures, he can help bring out each patient's sense of confidence and self-esteem," according to the website.

It goes on to say he meets with every prospective patient individually to discuss their expectations and what procedures will most likely produce the desired results. If he believes a person's expectations are not realistic, he will discourage them from having the procedure done. In addition, he fully informs the patient of all the risks involved in their surgeries and what to expect during and after plastic surgery, the website claims.

"I try to demystify plastic surgery," he adds. "That means erasing the fantasy, not giving a hard sell. I just try to make the patient . . . understand the procedure is not as difficult as they might imagine." In fact, the website says many patients express surprise after their surgery, saying that it was much easier than they ever believed it could be.

The website, dated 2005, has a description of a variety of procedures and brief explanations of what they do, as well as before-and-after pictures. The site lists eight ways a patient can pay for the surgery, from cash to traveler's checks, and states that financing is available.

Sally seemed to enjoy her new position. However, while Dr. Tucker was notably a good surgeon, there were some indications that he and Sally may have had some communication problems. When the Nursing Board investigator asked Sally what, if anything, she could have done wrong the day Sandra died, she said, "Not having better communication with Dr. Tucker. I'd go to him with problems and he didn't want to be bothered."

Other staff members at the center have been reluctant to talk about the working relationships in the office, so it is not known whether Dr. Tucker was difficult to work with in general, or if the atmosphere was strained only with Sally. It was said that he was constantly "nit-picking" about everything. However, when the North Carolina Medical Board investigated Sandra's death, Dr. Tucker and his office were found to be lax in everything from medication logs to methods for handling emergencies. Procedures were discovered to be, at best, sloppy. Medications were unaccounted for, some equipment didn't work properly and in at least one case, when a staff member was reprimanded, there was only a note about it, rather than an official document.

That was unthinkable to some. "Quite frankly, when a doctor doesn't want to be consulted about office procedures, it's because he's not comfortable looking after the problem himself, especially if there's an emergency," said a well-respected plastic surgeon who knows Dr. Tucker.

Still, there had not been any complaints lodged against

Dr. Tucker or Sally. While a couple of people mentioned that she was a bit of "an oddball," everyone seemed to think she was great at her job except for an early co-worker at Presbyterian Hospital who described Sally as "lazy" and said that she had a tendency to be a bit "heavy-handed" with medication. However, all of Sally's co-workers told the nursing board that they would have been comfortable with Sally as their nurse anesthetist before Sandra's death.

Sally's personal life was also going well. She and Jim moved into their dream house in 1989. The home had some land and was located in Weddington, North Carolina, about thirty minutes from Charlotte. The charming two-story brick house, which they purchased for around $78,000, had a wooded front yard and large backyard. They thought it would be ideal for children, but they never had any.

While Sandra's death and Sally's subsequent firing did not cause the couple to throw in the towel, it surely aggravated an already tense situation. In December 2005, before Sally was arrested and charged with Sandra's murder, the couple decided to go their separate ways.

"We had been to a couple of counselors, but we just have different beliefs. When my momma and daddy were ill and in a nursing home, I was under a lot of stress. He just wouldn't do anything to help me. I just felt like I couldn't take it any longer. I had been praying for my marriage for years, so when Jim said he wasn't happy, I felt like that was the answer to my prayers," Sally explained, admitting that she hadn't been happy either.

Jim moved out and Sally stayed in the house with the cats, including Winston, who had been Jim's cat for years.

Prior to their separation, Sally had developed some serious health problems. In April 2000 when she was 44, after suffering exhaustion and excessively heavy periods, Sally thought she might be starting menopause. Instead she was diagnosed with leukemia, a malignant cancer of the bone marrow and blood that is characterized by a lack of production of blood cells. An estimated 44,240 new cases are diagnosed every year in the U.S.

She was pale and experiencing constant fatigue that had nothing to do with sleep or rest. The fatigue, which is caused by anemia, also impairs the body's ability to fight infections, and prevents wounds and cuts from healing properly. The shortage of platelets results in bruising and easy bleeding. While the cause is not known, leukemia is often linked to chronic exposure to benzene and extraordinary doses of irradiation in the workplace.

"They caught it in time, so I could have outpatient chemotherapy treatments," she said.

The goal of treatment is to bring about a complete remission—in which case there should be no evidence of the disease and the patient returns to good health with the normal production of blood and marrow cells.

Not having a recurrence in five years is the best possible scenario. But in 2001, after Sandra's death, Sally had a relapse and had to be treated a second time.

"They couldn't give me chemotherapy again, so I had to drive to the doctor's office every day for arsenic treatments, which caused a lot of side effects," she recalled.

When Trisenox (arsenic trioxide) was first developed, it was intended for the treatment of rare diseases or conditions, but it had also been successful in treating people who have had relapses of cancer. Arsenic treatment had been used in the U.S. and Europe for over 100 years, until chemotherapy eventually replaced it. But recently, arsenic-based therapy has been revived. Reports indicated that 70 percent of patients who received the infusions were in remission within fifty-one days.

"I told them I didn't care about the side effects. At least I was alive, that's what counted. I know God has a plan."

Sally has remained under a doctor's care. No one knows if the leukemia will return again, but she is steadfast in her belief that it will not.

"I am healed in Jesus' name," she said emphatically.

Raised in a religious home, Sally had been involved in her church and practiced her faith for much of her life. At Good News Ministries, a small charismatic Christian church in Monroe, North Carolina, Sally worked with children in the nursery during services for several years, something she really enjoyed, especially as she felt it was helping the parents as well. But now there aren't enough families with small children to have a nursery, so Sally sits in with the pastor when he is counseling female church members.

"Reverend Ron [Jackson] always makes it a practice to have another church member in the room when he counsels a female," she explained, much like a doctor with an assistant on hand.

Her church and spirituality are a large part of Sally's life, especially since she has been on disability after Sandra's death. Sally's church friends have rallied around her since she was charged with Sandra's murder.

"She hasn't been able to work, she's had so much memory loss since the chemo," said Patty Campbell, a friend and nurse. "I feel so sorry for her, she's lost everything."

"She is a devout Christian with a good heart. . . . She always thinks of others," Diane Thomas, fellow church member, hairdresser and friend for over twenty-five years said. "She has such a forgiving heart. I was not there that day, so I can't say she didn't do this. But everything I know says she didn't have the heart to do this."

Sandy Stumpf, a retired nurse who worked with Sally at Presbyterian Hospital has said, "She was always a good nurse anesthetist. Sally is a precious person and a very committed Christian."

Everyone who knows Sally talks about what a natural-born nurturer she is.

"She is always the one who will send a card when someone is going through a hard time, or to thank them for their kindness. Sometimes she sends one just to say, 'Thinking of you,' " said Thomas.

Still, co-workers at the plastic surgery center told a Nursing Board investigator that Sally Hill stood in the back of the room eating a biscuit while Sandra Joyner was in respiratory arrest fighting for her life. They described her as "just standing there in a daze" doing nothing to help her patient.

The conflicting glimpses into Sally's life quite naturally cause speculation: who was the real Sally Hill—was she the caring person family and friends and church members knew . . . or did she have a dark side lurking just under the surface?

SIX

An Untimely Death

As far as anyone knew, Sandra and Sally had not seen each other since high school, except for that chance meeting in 1999 when Sandra had some minor work done by Dr. Tucker with Sally Hill administering the anesthetic.

"I was excited to see her," Sally said about her former classmate.

Sally told friends that Sandra didn't recognize her at first, that she'd had to remind Sandra that they had gone to school together. But then they spent some time reminiscing about their days at Olympic High.

However, Sally allegedly told a co-worker during that 1999 procedure, "That's the woman that stole my boyfriend." Nothing more was made of the statement at the time, but years later it would come back to haunt Sally.

Sandra had breezed through that first procedure. There were no complications during or after her surgery. Sandra's husband had picked her up after the procedure and cared for her for about a week while she recovered. It seemed logical that Sandra would return to Dr. Tucker when she decided to have several other procedures done in 2001.

Prior to the April 10 surgery, Sandra had made a preoperative visit to the center and completed all the necessary paperwork, including a health background and signed consent forms. On the history and physical sheets Sandra said that she had experienced mild chest pain along with anxiety and stress. She also said that she had not had an electrocardiogram performed in the previous twelve months and noted that she fainted easily. Still, she went into surgery without the EKG that would normally have been recommended, and a blood count that was slightly low, which didn't seem to be of concern to the doctor when Sally told him about it.

The day of Sandra's surgery started out like any other work day. Sally, who was scheduled to provide anesthesia for Sandra, was wearing some crisp scrubs, her hair held up with a clip. She arrived at the office around 6:50 a.m., to set up her medications for the day and get the operating room ready. She reviewed the patient's case to refresh her memory and to make sure she hadn't overlooked anything.

It had already been determined that heavy IV sedation would be the anesthesia for Sandra's facelift and other procedures. Sally checked the anesthesia machine and got the drugs she would need for the day's surgeries from the locked storage cabinet. Under law, someone was supposed to witness the narcotics being taken from the storage area and the drugs being entered into the logbook. At the end of the day, all of the medication was supposed to be accounted for and documented. But on this day, that never happened.

As Sally prepared for the surgery, the doctor's nurse confirmed that Sandra had followed instructions, she had not had anything to eat or drink since midnight.

The nurse also asked about any allergies, but Sandra didn't mention any. Sally then went over the procedures that would be done that day to make sure Sandra had not changed her mind about any of them.

Once in her gown, Sandra was taken to the operating room, where Dr. Tucker marked the areas on her face where he would be operating.

Sandra was then in Sally's hands.

With the pulse oximeter attached to Sandra's forefinger, and the EKG and blood pressure monitors turned on, the IV drip, which was infused with fentanyl and Versed (like Valium), was inserted into the back of Sandra's left hand and her arm placed on the armrest at her side. In less than thirty seconds, Sandra was out.

The importance of the pulse oximeter was always stressed—it could literally be a lifesaver. "It's the greatest invention there ever was," said Cindy Martin, a Chapel Hill nurse anesthesiologist. "The brain and heart and lungs are oxygen hogs," she added. "The body will take oxygen away from the finger before a person dies. If the finger is getting one hundred percent oxygen, the brain is getting one hundred percent." An alarm is designed to go off if the blood oxygen drops below a set limit, say 80 percent.

In some instances the pulse oximeter may fall off of a patient's finger, but if it does, the situation is easily remedied by wrapping tape around it to hold it on the finger, according to several nurse anesthetists.

As the surgery progresses, the fentanyl is bumped up periodically in order to keep the patient under sedation; however, it is important that it is only increased ½ cc at a time. The patient is getting oxygen through the nose as her vitals are being carefully monitored.

Generally an assistant and the nurse anesthetist are in the operating room with the surgeon, as well as a scrub technician and circulating nurse who is in and out getting supplies as they are needed. Typically the nurse anesthetist sits at the patient's head watching the surgery and the monitors. Sometimes music plays softly in the background.

When the surgery is complete, the patient is allowed to come out from under the anesthesia for about five minutes before being moved to a bed. She remains there—still being constantly monitored—for a few minutes before she is moved to a wheelchair and taken to the recovery room. As the patient becomes more alert, she is asked if she would like a cracker or some ginger ale. At that point the catheter is removed.

According to Sally's notes, everything was routine before and during Sandra's surgery that morning. At 7 a.m., Sandra was given two pre-operative medications (Valium and Zofran) to help her relax.

At 7:15 a.m., IV fluids, which included an antibiotic, were started. Sally made a notation that Sandra had mentioned that she was nervous, which was not unusual for a patient right before any surgery.

By 7:40 Sandra was in the operating room and an infusion of anesthesia medications was begun. Sally noted that the surgery began at 8:27 a.m., and ended at 11:00 a.m.

Dr. Tucker anticipated it would take three and a half to four hours to complete the mini-facelift, fat grafting and injections into two scars and lips, and then the laser resurfacing. Sally sat on a stool near Sandra's head to adjust the IV and monitor her throughout the procedures.

Dr. Tucker began by making a small incision over Sandra's left ear. He gently pulled the skin and fascia underneath, angling it up toward her hairline to smooth out her jaw and cheek line. He was careful not to pull too tightly.

Once he had positioned the skin in the right place, Dr. Tucker carefully removed the excess tissue and sutured the incision, which would be well-hidden by Sandra's hair. He then repeated the procedure on the right side, making sure both sides were symmetrical. The mini-facelift, which would have a faster recovery period than a traditional full lift, since it wasn't as invasive, was completed in a little over an hour and a half.

Dr. Tucker then began the process of retrieving some fat from Sandra's abdomen that would be used to fill in a couple of scars and to plump up her lips to make them look fuller. A person's own body fat mixed with a commercial filler product was the most natural way to fill in and even out scars and indentations. Then, using a fine gauge needle, Dr. Tucker injected the fat and filler into a scar on her forehead and another along her jawline. It took a little longer to fill in her lips since they had to be manipulated to ensure a natural look before the filler set.

The final procedure was laser therapy on her lower eyelids to smooth out under-eye lines caused by the environment, which Sandra thought made her look tired all the time.

Laser technology, which has become one of the most promising—and popular—weapons against aging, is far less traumatic to the skin than full-blown surgery. Basically, the laser vaporizes superficial layers of skin, removing wrinkles and lines caused by sun damage and facial expressions.

At 11:10 a.m. Sally added a notation at the bottom of the anesthesia record documenting the last set of vital signs that were taken in the operating room. Sandra's blood pressure was 109/93; pulse 99; respiration 16, and O_2 saturation was 96 percent, all of which were normal. Her skin was warm to the touch and her color good. Sally then noted that Sandra had been transferred to the recovery room in a wheelchair. According to records, her patient was admitted to the recovery room at 11:15 a.m.

Sandra remained in a wheelchair, but was reportedly awake and oriented to her surroundings. There was a note saying that she was restless and complaining of facial pain. The notation was not signed.

Once in the recovery room, Sandra was able to get out of the wheelchair on her own and was helped into the large recliner, where she would remain, drifting in and out of sleep for a couple of hours. Still in a surgical gown with her face bandaged, Sandra was covered with a light-weight blanket, and ice packs were positioned on her eyes to keep the swelling down. She was talking to the nurses as they helped her get settled in.

The recovery room patient was supposed to be hooked up to a blood pressure monitor and pulse oximeter that would gauge oxygen intake. It could literally be a life-saver, because an alarm would sound if the patient's oxygen saturation dropped too low.

Technically Sally's job was finished once the patient was in the recovery room; at that point she was supposed to go to the front and get the next patient. But this partic-ular day the recovery room nurse asked Sally to stand in for her while she went down the hall for a few minutes.

Typically it was the responsibility of the recovery room nurse to check vital signs every fifteen minutes and to record them on the chart. The nurse was also supposed to observe the patient to make sure there were not any changes in her condition.

Sally seemed to like to work in the recovery room, and continued to stand in, even though she had been repri-manded earlier by a superior for staying in the recovery room too long, since it wasn't really part of her responsi-bility. She had also been cautioned about giving medica-tions there.

Within minutes after getting settled in, Sandra started to complain of pain in her face, which was not surprising, since so much of the work done had been around her eyes and mouth. The pain medication she had been given in the IV during surgery was also beginning to wear off by then.

Records show that at 11:20 a.m. Sandra received 2 ccs of IV fentanyl, a fast-acting pain medication, after complaining that her lower eyelids and face were hurting, both administered by Sally Hill while the recovery room nurse was admitting the next patient, according to Sally's notes.

"My face hurts, it feels like it's on fire," Sandra complained.

Casually, as she had done so many other times, Sally stepped into the hall where she kept her supply cart and retrieved a syringe with 1 cc of fentanyl and gave it to Sandra.

It was just a few minutes until Sandra complained again, saying that the pain medication wasn't helping. By then she was drawing her knees up to her chest in pain.

"Am I being a bad patient?" she asked.

"No, of course not," Sally reassured her.

Sally gave Sandra the second 1 cc dose of fentanyl. It had been five minutes since she had given the first injection.

Sally apparently then stepped across the hall to the break room to get a bite to eat and some coffee. One of the doctors had brought in Bojangles biscuits for everyone. The nurses often grabbed a bite to eat on the run when they had a full schedule; however, someone was supposed to be in the recovery room watching the patient at all times.

Four or five nurses were thought to be working in the clinic that day. It was during the time when Sally was out of the room that one of the other nurses passing through noticed that Sandra's color had changed, her lips had a bluish cast. At first the nurse wasn't alarmed, she thought it might be because of the fat grafts to Sandra's lips, which could cause bruising. But when she walked around to the other side of the recliner to take a closer look, she could see that Sandra's fingernails were also bluish, indicating oxygen deprivation.

"Sandra, Sandra," the nurse called.

When there was no response, the nurse pinched Sandra's toe, trying to get her to respond. When there was no response, the nurse immediately pushed back the recliner, while another nurse grabbed an oxygen mask and pressed it to Sandra's face.

"Take a deep breath," she urged.

Sandra responded immediately and began to breathe normally just as Sally was walking back into the room.

"Is she OK?" one of the nurses asked Sally.

"She's fine," Sally replied.

The nurse then went on about her duties.

But seconds later, when the regular recovery room nurse returned to her post, she immediately noticed that Sandra's O_2 saturation and blood pressure had dropped to 81.

It was later discovered that, for some unknown reason, the alarm on the pulse oximeter, which should have sounded when Sandra's oxygen level dropped dangerously low, had allegedly been turned off. It would have alerted the staff that Sandra was in danger of going into respiratory arrest.

However, it was clear that Sandra's condition had drastically deteriorated. In fact, the coroner later determined that she had stopped breathing after the second injection of fentanyl.

While concerned for Sandra, everyone acquiesced to Sally, who was still in charge of the patient.

"Do you want someone to get Dr. Tucker?" a nurse asked, since the doctor was supposed to be notified any time there was a change in a patient's condition.

"No, everything is fine," Sally replied.

Seconds later, when another nurse saw Sally go into the operating room, she again asked if Sally needed any help.

"I have more help than I need today," she snapped back.

Sally continued to go about her business as she always did. There didn't appear to be any sense of urgency as she got a pre-mixed syringe of Robinul and ephedrine—Robinul to regulate the heart and ephedrine to dilate the bronchial tubes. It was customary for Sally to keep such a syringe ready in case there was a problem. But even after she gave the injection, there was no change in Sandra's condition.

Now alarmed, one of the nurses hurried to get Dr. Tucker, who was in the room next door. He ran immediately to the recovery room where the staff was hovering over Sandra.

The air was thick, as though everything was happening in slow motion. Dr. Tucker and the staff—everyone except Sally—worked feverishly to intubate Sandra to open her airways and try to resuscitate her.

There was no change.

His pulse quickening, Dr. Tucker began to do compressions on her. It was then he yelled at the staff to get Sandra on the floor so he could use the paddles.

Still no change.

"Do you want me to call 911?" one of the nurses asked.

"Yes!" he ordered.

At 11:35 a.m., just twenty minutes after Sandra's plastic surgery had been completed, the police and EMTs were on the way.

It was a stark scene when they arrived and saw Sandra's lifeless body.

"It was obvious that she had coded, but no one seemed

upset," said one of the EMTs who arrived on the scene and began CPR. "Everyone seemed very calm. Even the doctor wasn't excited."

The EMT and a police officer lifted Sandra from the bed onto a gurney. "She wasn't breathing. We ventilated her with a bag mask and began compressions," he later recalled. He said her color indicated that she had stopped breathing in the last ten to twelve minutes.

It was a scene he said would be etched into his memory forever. It was so surreal compared to the horrible accidents and chaos he was used to seeing on a regular basis. "It was wild seeing someone that young who had coded in an office after plastic surgery."

EMS providers arrived at the center at 11:57 a.m. Though there is no record of what time they were called or how long it took to get there, reports indicated that it was a four-mile trip from the dispatch site. The EMTs rushed Sandra to the nearest medical facility, Carolinas Medical Center-Mercy hospital. En route the paramedics administered Narcan, a drug used to counteract the effects of an overdose of pain medication.

The EMS providers first documented Sandra's vital signs at 12:10 p.m., indicating that she had a blood pressure and pulse but was being artificially ventilated. Her pupils were dilated and she was unresponsive, according to their notes.

In their report the EMS workers said that in the recovery room Sandra's oxygen saturation rates had dropped to 20 and her blood pressure (systolic) was down to 60. She had a decrease in responsiveness and had suffered respiratory arrest. There was no mention of the timing of these events in the EMS records, or in any documentation that the center provided.

Records show that Sandra was admitted to the hospital at 12:25 p.m., still unresponsive.

There was no further documentation on the patient's chart recorded by Sally (the day of Sandra's death), but according to at least one news report, after leaving the hospital, the staff went back to the office to try and document what happened after Sandra went into respiratory arrest.

Once Sandra was at the hospital, doctors worked feverishly trying to revive her. Her next of kin, listed as emergency contacts on Dr. Tucker's paperwork, were called and told there had been complications after her surgery. Sandra's mother and sister had no other information when they arrived at the hospital.

For the remainder of the day a team of doctors ran batteries of tests, MRIs, brain scans, and blood tests to determine the extent of her coma. The hospital laboratory work showed evidence of acidosis, and an EEG revealed findings consistent with a major anoxic encephalopathy disorder, a severe lack of oxygen to the brain.

For the next five days Sandra remained in a deep coma. Neurological evaluations indicated that the prognosis was grave, since there was evidence that Sandra had severe and irreversible brain damage.

Five days later the family gave the hospital permission to harvest her organs, and Sandra was removed from life support and pronounced dead.

The medical examiner determined that Sandra had died from an overdose of pain medication, which had caused respiratory arrest and coma. While tragic, he ruled it had been a terrible accident.

It was not until much later—after medical and nursing board hearings—that it was determined that Dr. Tucker and Sally Hill's substandard care had caused Sandra to suffer severe physical injury, and to eventually die because of her injuries.

"How can a woman who has never been sick a day in

her life go into surgery perfectly healthy and come out in a vegetative state?" John kept asking over and over.

It was the question on everyone's mind: How could things have gone so terribly wrong?

SEVEN

Good-byes

John Joyner was oblivious to the mild and sunny days outside of Mercy Hospital, where for five days and nights he sat by Sandra's side, waiting for a miracle.

The morning of Sandra's surgery, he had gotten the kids off to school and then gone to work.

He had felt good about the family's visit the night before. They had all been glad they were able to have some quality time together. In many ways it had seemed like old times for them.

When the kids got home from school that afternoon, they asked John if he had heard from their mom.

"I hadn't, but I wasn't concerned. I told them Sandra's mom and sister had probably taken her home and were taking care of her," he recalled. It wasn't until late that night, after everyone had gone to bed, that he would learn the truth.

It was about 11 p.m. when John got a call from Sandra's sister Debbie, who was on her cell phone, sitting in his driveway. She asked him to come downstairs.

Something had gone terribly wrong and Sandra was in a coma, Debbie told him. John was in shock. He didn't wake the boys, he left them sleeping. He didn't really grasp how desperate the situation was until he got to the hospital less than thirty minutes later. Even then he couldn't comprehend what the medical staff was trying to tell him, that Sandra was brain-dead.

"When I walked in, they told me Sandra's condition was without any hope. I was in disbelief. It was so bizarre—it came out of left field," he recalled.

"Sandra was basically brain-dead, asphyxiated. Sandra lost consciousness and the medical staff couldn't revive her. There's only so long the brain can go without oxygen; after three of four minutes, the person is brain-dead," he added. "There were so many things being thrown at me, I was just trying to understand."

For five days John sat by Sandra's side around the clock at the hospital watching her lifeless body. He rubbed her and talked to her as the nurses had told him to do.

He watched her blood pressure go up, then down, and back up again. Her heart would beat normally for a while, then it would be off the charts. Some days her coloring would be better, and he would see her body twitch, all of which made him hopeful again.

"I loved her. Sitting there with her, it was like watching my whole life pass before me." Various people tried to talk to him about organ donation, but he couldn't deal with that subject yet.

"They told me there was no way the damage would be reversible, but I just didn't want to believe it."

Frantic, he got second and third opinions; people called to tell him about someone they had known who had come out of a coma.

"But the doctors and nurses kept saying that wasn't possible in this case, that the lack of oxygen to the brain is the worst. The people who had brain trauma that put them into unconsciousness were in a vegetative state; once they had oxygen deprivation, they weren't coming back," he explained.

He just couldn't grasp the finality of it all.

"I don't understand how a perfectly healthy woman who has never even had a cold or the flu could go into surgery and come out in a vegetative state," he wondered.

"The brain can't go without oxygen, it dies in three to four minutes," he repeated as if still trying to convince himself.

Every day John struggled to understand that Sandra would never come back.

"I'm a manager of a big company. I just figured I could fix anything; nothing really bad had ever happened."

He thought of the Terri Schiavo case and the battle her parents had waged to keep her alive. But he knew that Sandra wouldn't want that, stuck in bed, barely garbling her words. Still, he couldn't give up.

"I told the doctors I made good money, that I could get all the hospital equipment that was needed and take her home, I could put her in the living room and get twenty-four-hour-a-day nursing care for her."

The doctors weren't even sure they could keep Sandra alive on the machines for another twenty-four hours.

More than anything John's heart was broken for their sons Philip and Grayson. By then he had told the boys that their mother's prognosis was not good. He didn't want them to see her in a vegetative state; he hadn't been able to tell them yet that there was no hope for her.

"It was a horrible thing to experience. There is nothing in the world that can prepare you to ever have to go home and tell your two kids that their mother is not going to be back."

Sandra had devoted her life to her children, and everyone said there wasn't a better mother anywhere.

"That's the real tragedy, she was such a great mother to them and they loved her so incredibly. They had always been so close, they deserved to have their mother. It was such a raw deal, it was the worst thing in the world that could happen to them."

So many hearts were broken when family and friends learned that Sandra had died after plastic surgery.

"She was Olympic High School, she was such a part of our high school years. She always had such promise. I broke down and cried when I heard the news," said high school friend Mark Perry.

Gregg Pence, another Olympic High classmate, had reconnected with Sandra a few months earlier. When he arrived at work Monday morning, his employee Jimmy Niell—the infamous "chick magnet" at the heart of the murder/grudge theory—asked if Gregg had heard about Sandra Baker. Gregg didn't know what Jimmy was talking about.

"I saw it on the news, she had some plastic surgery and she's in a coma," he told Gregg.

Gregg had been seeing Sandra for about five months, having dinner and drinks, meeting up at tailgate parties, reminiscing about old times at Olympic High. A brief encounter had brought them together in the fall of 2000.

Gregg was at The Sunset Club in Charlotte's popular South End, sitting at the bar having a cocktail when he saw someone standing at the door peering in. It was Sandra; she was by herself. They waved to each other across the room, and she came in and joined him at the bar and ordered a drink.

In their hour-long conversation, Sandra mentioned to him that she and John were separated, which he had not heard. To this day he believes she told him about the separation because she didn't want him to think she was still married and out running around.

Gregg says she had apparently been to the club before, maybe with girlfriends, because the bartender seemed to know her.

"She was the same bubbly and bright person she was in high school. She looked the same, she didn't appear to have a problem in the world," he recalled.

They agreed to get together—for old times' sake—and exchanged phone numbers. But she was quick to clarify that she didn't date, they would just be getting together as friends.

A couple of weeks into October, Gregg called her and they met for a cocktail. For the next few months they would see each other almost every weekend, taking walks in Freedom Park, or he would cook at his house. Sometimes they would put on some soul music and dance.

Gregg invited her to a couple of parties he gave with neighbors; she fit right in. They met at a Carolina Panthers tailgate party, but when it was time for the kickoff, they would sit with their respective friends who had seats.

Sandra talked a lot about her kids, but only mentioned John once.

The only time Gregg ever saw her sad was when she came over to his house for a Super Bowl party in 2001. She brought a bottle of champagne, which was her favorite, and a couple of balloons for the occasion. But then she left at halftime, saying she wasn't having a good day.

"John and my sons are at the house watching the game together," she said sadly.

On a couple of occasions Gregg and Sandra met at The Palm, which was within walking distance of her apartment at Post Park; however, Gregg says he was never inside her apartment; they always met somewhere else.

According to Gregg, just before her death, Sandra had landed a part-time job as a hostess at Upstream, an upscale seafood restaurant in Phillips Place.

"She was having fun, she had been tied down for twenty-five years and had raised two sons," Gregg said. "She was a knockout—blonde hair, red lips, gold jewelry—and driving a little white Mercedes convertible. Even Ray Charles couldn't miss her," he quipped.

Gregg was impressed with the fact that Sandra had a lot of close girlfriends. She would often talk about what was going on in their lives. One time when she was at his house for cocktails and hors d'oeuvres, one of her friends called, upset.

"Sandra needed to leave to comfort her girlfriend, so I went with her," he recalled.

Gregg's face brightens when he thinks back to how much Sandra loved her new model Mercedes Coupé. One night after they had had dinner at his house, she took him for a spin in it.

"She was driving sixty miles an hour up Scaleybark, a quiet neighborhood street; she was screaming, 'Isn't this fun?' "

Ironically, while John thought Sandra was depressed and struggling with the changes in her life, Gregg found Sandra to be happy, having a good time being on her own. Some of her girlfriends have said she was enjoying herself so much that she wasn't even considering reconciling with John, although he was still holding out hope.

Although Gregg suspected that Sandra may have had other men interested in her, she never mentioned anyone. They just enjoyed each other's company. They had developed a solid friendship that might eventually turn into something more, he thought. "But we weren't boyfriend and girlfriend," he added quickly. "I think she was intrigued by me, the fact that I had been single all these years, that I had a nice home and had built a good business," explained Gregg, who has never married and isn't even sure he has ever been in love.

"But I sure did think a lot of Sandra," he said thoughtfully. "Any guy would consider Sandra a great catch."

However, an acquaintance who hung out with the Palm

group and had been to Sandra's house for a party described her as a woman "looking for love in all the wrong places."

It was not uncommon to see Sandra sipping a champagne cocktail at The Palm by herself. "She always dressed great and looked perfect," said another Palm regular. "She wouldn't go out unless she was looking her best."

Some people said she had become involved with a "gigolo type," a good-looking man who, even when married or involved in a relationship, always seemed to have another woman on the side, generally someone with money.

A few years earlier he had met a wealthy older woman while traveling and moved in with her. She set him up with a local restaurant, but eventually the relationship soured and he began dating a younger woman whom he later married.

But while he was courting the younger woman, he was also seeing Sandra—and she was falling for him and his charms, say acquaintances.

"We heard rumors that Sandra caused his girlfriend to have a miscarriage because she was harassing her," said one acquaintance. "She lived close to the salon where his girlfriend worked. She would supposedly go in there and leave her letters and phone messages that upset her," the woman said. The ladies' man has since moved with his wife (his former girlfriend) out of the country.

"It was sad, it was obvious she was lonely and trying to make friends. She would call me over and over trying to get together, she was so lonely," said an acquaintance who would see her often.

Friends who knew Sandra well tried to help her find her way. Scott Redd, who had known Sandra since high school, asked Linda Seligman, a friend in the wine business, to take her along on her wine distributor route so Sandra could learn the business.

"I wanted her to see the day-to-day workings, to make

sure it was something she was really interested in. I didn't have an opening at the time, but I thought riding with Linda for a couple of days would let her know if it was something she was really interested in."

During the holidays, Scott, Linda and their dates went to a Christmas party at Sandra's along with twenty-five others. The two-bedroom condo with a loft was beautifully decorated with a huge tree and other holiday accessories, and Sandra was in a festive mood.

Scott and his girlfriend invited Sandra to go with them to some other holiday parties, which she seemed to enjoy. But after the holidays she just seemed to disappear.

Scott became a sounding board for Sandra in the months after her separation.

"I knew she was unhappy when she moved out. She was having a hard time. She didn't talk much about what caused the separation, but she talked about her boys constantly," he said. "She really missed her boys and her home."

Occasionally acquaintances would see her with someone at The Palm, but more often than not she was stewing about why things hadn't worked out with the one she wanted, the married man from Morocco.

"She liked him a lot and it didn't work out. She was upset about it," said a friend she discussed the situation with. "I told her, 'As good looking as you are, you can have anyone you want.'"

But she didn't seem to be able to forget about it. She was high-strung and anxious, and on top of that, had a flair for the dramatic, says the friend.

"Any time we ran into each other, she wanted to talk about the failed relationship. She kept asking, 'What's his problem?' She was worried about what kind of work she might be able to get into and how she could get her life back together," the friend added.

"She was down, she wanted to meet somebody. I tried to tell her to just give it time. I would say, 'You just got separated, things will take time.' She was definitely troubled."

At one point, she was so discouraged, she told him, "I can't work anything out with anyone," referring to her failed marriage and the relationship with the charmer.

After the first of the year, Sandra dropped out of sight.

Early in April, Gregg had asked her to go to a Billy Joel/Elton John concert. "She said she would love to, but that she already had plans."

The plans, it turned out, were to recover from a mini-facelift and some other cosmetic work.

Sandra was buried Wednesday, April 18, at Magnolia Memorial Gardens. The service was held at 11 a.m. and officiated by Dr. E. Glenn Wagner at Calvary Church on Pineville–Matthews Road, where Sandra's parents were parishioners.

That day the church auditorium was packed with family and friends offering their condolences to Sandra's parents Roy and Betty Baker, her sister Deborah and husband Robert Stuck, and John, Grayson and Philip, who were beside themselves over their loss.

A striking photo of Sandra with her light-up-a-room smile graced the cover of the memorial program. Inside was a lament from Mrs. Baker entitled "From a Mother's Heart."

She wrote:

My Dearest, Dearest Sandra:

It would take volumes to write about you. It thrills my heart to know God looked around Heaven and decided that you were the special little girl for your Dad and I . . . So He sent you so we could love and care for you. We loved every stage of your life. You were one of the best Mothers ever. We had such a bond as you raised Grayson and Philip. I watched you, and if a Mother ever loved her children, you did and truly gave your heart and life to their care.

This past week God decided He needed you back with Him so in His timing and love He took you home. I am so happy and thankful to have had you for all these years. You'll be waiting for me on the portals of heaven, and we'll be together forever with our Lord Jesus Christ. Until then, I will cherish all the love and wonderful memories you gave us. Truly it is not good bye . . . but wait for me Sandra . . . I'll see you soon.

As ever, all my love,
Mother

On a gray afternoon, with temperatures cooler than normal for springtime, Sandra's family and friends huddled to stay warm and to comfort each other. Sandra Baker Joyner, with only half of her life lived, was laid to rest in Magnolia Memorial Gardens in Calvary Church's six-acre cemetery.

The evening before the funeral Gregg had gone to the viewing at the Calvary Church chapel, which was filled with relatives and friends, many of whom had known Sandra at Olympic High. Afterwards Gregg returned to one of their old haunts, The Palm, where they had had some good times together.

This time he sat at the bar alone, nursing a cocktail, with only his memories to keep him company.

EIGHT

Medical Findings

According to the medical examiner, Sandra Joyner died at 3:45 p.m. on Sunday, April 15. In his opinion, the cause of death was lack of oxygen, which had resulted in respiratory failure. The report said that Sandra had initially suffered toxicity from too much pain medication, which had then caused complications.

Her death was ruled an accidental poisoning by medication.

Clearly several factors had played a role in her death: the medication toxicity, most likely due to fentanyl—which she had been given in the operating room and twice in the recovery room after complaining that she was in pain—the hypoxic brain injury and respiratory arrest.

The report went on to say that before the surgery, Sandra had appeared to be healthy, and that there had been no evidence of any existing disease, although there appeared to be some pneumonia in one of her lungs, which may have been caused by aspiration.

The medical examiner determined that, after the plastic surgery procedures were completed, Sandra had had an increase in blood pressure and then went into respiratory failure, followed by hypoxic/ischemic brain injury with cerebral swelling.

According to the medical examiner, during surgery Sandra had been given fenzodiazepine (a tranquilizer) and fentanyl under local anesthesia, without any complication. Once she had gone into respiratory arrest and couldn't be revived, she had been given Robinul and ephedrine, and later she was given Narcan to offset the overdose.

It may not have been possible to determine when Sandra had been given the Narcan, the antidote to reverse the effects of the pain medication, but the timing might turn out to be critical. The medical examiner said that the reason for the initial increase in blood pressure and respiratory depression was not clear; however, it was thought that it could be due to the adverse effect and interaction of the medications, including the fentanyl.

A website that contains questions and answers about the drug lists several conditions that could cause negative reactions to fentanyl, which include:

— An infection
— High or low blood pressure
— Lung disease or breathing difficulties
— Other medicines, sulfites, foods, dyes or preservatives

The site also lists twenty-six drugs that might negatively interact with fentanyl including: antidepressant drugs called MAOIs; erythromycin; fluconazole; herbal products including St. John's wort; ketoconazole; medicines for diarrhea, high blood pressure and seizures; other strong medicines for pain; and rifampin.

The website warns that fentanyl may cause drowsiness, so other medications that will also cause the same symptom should be avoided, including alcohol and alcohol-containing medicines, barbiturates such as phenobarbital, certain antidepressants or tranquilizers, muscle relaxants and some antihistamines often used in cold medicines.

The site points out that prior to surgery a patient should always tell his or her healthcare professional about any prescription or nonprescription medications, nutritional supplements or herbal products he or she is taking. In fact it is important to stop some of them two to three weeks before surgery. The patient should also let the physician's office know if he or she frequently ingests caffeine or alcohol, smoke, or use illegal drugs.

In addition, product literature states that it is critical for the patient to tell the healthcare provider if pain continues after being given fentanyl, or if it gets worse or is a different type of pain than he or she had before.

Side effects of fentanyl that require medical attention are mentioned, including: breathing difficulties and wheezing, slow or fast heartbeat, unusual weakness, confusion, light-headedness or fainting spells, and nervousness or restlessness.

Other symptoms that can occur but do not need medical attention are dizziness and drowsiness, dry mouth, flushing, headache, nausea and vomiting, and sweating.

A urine screen done before Sandra's surgery indicated that she had fenzodiazepine (a Valium-type drug) and Zofram (another relaxant) in her system, but there were no signs of barbiturates, cocaine, opiates or any type of amphetamine. The medical examiner noted that the drugs found in the sample would have been in her system the night before.

Sandra's husband believed that she had been taking an antidepressant after they separated, but that was not mentioned specifically in the report.

In the medical examiner's opinion there could have been a rebound effect—meaning that more of the drug would be required for the same effect in the future—with the fentanyl, and he speculated that it may have coincided with the post-operative administration of the pain medication.

Puncture marks from intravenous catheters and IVs, as well as bruising from the surgery and subsequent intervention efforts were noted in the report, all of which were normal under the circumstances. There was also evidence of organ donation, which the family had agreed upon before Sandra was taken off life support.

Clearly Sandra's life should not have ended the way it did. Something—or several unexplainable things—had gone terribly wrong after her surgery. It had been a horrible combination of circumstances, something people seldom consider when having "routine" plastic surgery.

The American Association of Plastic Surgeons estimates that more than 11 million men and women have plastic surgery and cosmetic procedures a year, yet there is a less than one percent complication rate in office-based plastic surgery procedures done across the country every day.

"But surgery is surgery; whether it's done in an office or hospital, there's an inherent risk," said a Charlotte plastic surgeon who has practiced for decades. "But if there is a problem, it is generally with the anesthetic, even though plastic surgery patients, on the whole, are generally very healthy and seldom react to anesthesia."

With less than one percent of plastic and cosmetic surgery patients experiencing complications of any kind, unfortunately, Sandra Joyner was the exception to the rule.

NINE

Dr. Tucker

At 46, Dr. Peter Loren Tucker was just a year older than Sandra at the time of her surgery and subsequent death. He had been in private practice for nine years and was a popular surgeon. He received his medical degree from Wake Forest University's Bowman Gray medical school in Winston-Salem, North Carolina, in 1981. He went on to do a year of postgraduate work at the University of Tennessee in Chattanooga in 1982, followed by a second postgraduate program from 1982 to 1987.

He worked with Charlotte's Presbyterian Hospital for several years, then joined the practice with doctors Laird and Giblin before going into private practice.

Dr. Tucker's résumé does not specify whether his internship at the University of Tennessee was in plastic surgery. The university has acknowledged that Dr. Tucker was there from 1981 to 1987, but wasn't able to locate any other information about his specialty.

However, Thomas Mansfield, attorney for the North Carolina Medical Board, said it is likely that Dr. Tucker's internship had, in fact, been in plastic surgery since he'd obtained a Tennessee medical license in 1981 to practice plastic surgery, and then gotten a North Carolina license in 1987 before moving to Charlotte.

But at least one medical practitioner questioned the quality of Dr. Tucker's schooling, saying he may have been "thinly trained," because the program he participated in was not included among the top five medical schools at the time: Harvard University, Johns Hopkins University, Washington University in St. Louis, the University of Pennsylvania and the University of California at San Francisco.

There is a distinct difference between a plastic surgeon trained to perform breast augmentations, rhinoplasty and liposuction, and one who has been trained to perform corrective surgery like repairing a cleft palate or reconstructing a jaw after it has been smashed in an automobile accident.

Peers who have been trained to perform complex surgery on birth defects or horrible injuries, for instance, believe there is a difference in attitude when they are dealing with someone who could be in a life-or-death situation.

"Someone who is trained to care for sick people will be extra careful to make sure the patient doesn't get into any trouble during surgery," said one doctor.

Regardless, becoming a plastic surgeon is not an easy career choice. After obtaining an undergraduate degree, an aspiring plastic surgeon must then complete four years of medical school. There are then three years of residency required, though residency can last for as many as five to seven years. Ultimately, an accredited plastic surgeon in the U.S. must also be certified by The American Board of Plastic Surgery.

The residency period is examined by the board, and the evaluation must be satisfactory before the resident is allowed to train specifically in plastic surgery. The process is then followed by written and oral exams.

Surprisingly, within the U.S., it is legal for any doctor, regardless of specialty, to perform cosmetic surgery. Plastic surgery is recognized by the American Board of Medical Specialties as a subspecialty dedicated to the surgical repair of defects of form or function, including cosmetic or aesthetic surgery, as well as reconstructive surgery.

The term "cosmetic surgery," however, refers to surgery that is designed to improve cosmetics or appearance. In several countries, including Australia, many doctors who are not qualified as surgeons can perform cosmetic procedures.

When Dr. Tucker first arrived in Charlotte he worked at Presbyterian Hospital, then in 1995 he joined an existing practice with two other plastic surgeons; in 1997 he decided to open his own practice.

At the time of Sandra's death, all of Dr. Tucker's credentials were in order. He was board-certified and had hospital privileges at Charlotte's three major hospitals: Carolinas Medical Center, Mercy Hospital and Presbyterian Hospital.

Dr. Tucker, who is about 5 feet 9 inches tall, with a bit of a paunch that he blames on the fact that he quit smoking for a while, is soft-spoken and personable. His short reddish blonde hair, which matches his ruddy complexion, is often hidden under a surgical cap. It is not unusual to see him in the office any time of day, wearing his scrubs rather than a white coat.

Some potential clients who have had consultations with him say they found Dr. Tucker a little overly solicitous, but patients who have known him for years find him delightful and say, "He just loves women."

In spite of the tragedy he continues to have some loyal, long-term patients who are happy with his work and feel confident that Sally Hill, alone, was responsible for Sandra's death.

Crissy, ex-wife of famous wrestler Ric Flair, still goes

to Dr. Tucker for Botox. Beauty expert Debra Kennedy, whom Dr. Tucker's office sponsors in her beauty business venture, is also a loyal patient, but neither would go on the record to endorse him, even to attest to his surgical skills.

Dr. Tucker's office is located on the first floor of a nondescript medical building at 300 Billingsley Road, along with a couple of eye doctors, a dentist and other MDs.

Before opening his own practice, Dr. Tucker was in partnership with Dr. Giblin and Dr. Laird, but it is not known if he was an equal partner. Both are now retired. According to one doctor, Dr. Laird had his own problems at the time.

One story continues to circulate about an emergency that occurred while a patient was being kept overnight after a liposuction procedure performed by Dr. Laird. When the patient began having blood pressure problems and the nurse on duty wasn't able to reach Dr. Laird, she felt it was in the patient's best interest to send her to the hospital. When Dr. Laird learned that the nurse had admitted his patient to the hospital without his approval, he was reportedly irate.

"He was verbally abusive and hurled racial slurs" at the nurse, who was African-American, recalls one doctor. Sally's delay in notifying Dr. Tucker when Sandra was in trouble caused some to wonder if she was reluctant to bring a problem to Dr. Tucker's attention, and if that could have been why she'd tried to rectify the situation on her own without getting Dr. Tucker involved.

Dr. Tucker's office suite is a cut above the standard doctor's office. The waiting room has three areas, one with a fireplace. Rich, dark wood columns and cabinets provide a warm look, rather than the usual cold steel office furniture.

Generally five nurses work at Dr. Tucker's office, one of whom is the nurse anesthetist. A business card available at the front desk lists his wife Lynn Tucker as the business manager.

A gold business card available for the taking contains general information about the practice and a description of various plastic surgery procedures, ranging from rhinoplasty to breast implants.

Sometimes Dr. Tucker prefers to greet potential patients in the waiting room rather than the exam room. He shakes hands with them and escorts them down the hall to the room where he will do the consult. His assistant accompanies them and remains in the room throughout the meeting, which lasts about forty minutes.

According to one potential new client who approached Dr. Tucker in 2007 about some rejuvenation work, he was very complimentary, telling her she certainly didn't look her age, which was 60.

He commented on her beautiful blue eyes, asking if she wore contacts.

"You must have good genes," he continued.

"What concerns you most, what procedure are you interested in having done?" he asked the potential client, much like the plastic surgeons on the hit TV show *Nip/Tuck*.

"The lines around my mouth, especially the ones at the corners."

Those, he explained, are called marionette lines; they are separate from the folds along the sides of the mouth.

He had her stand and face the mirror. She slipped off her shoes so she would be at eye level with him, as she was the taller of the two. He stood behind her so they could both see her reflection in the mirror and he gently pulled back her lower face and upper neck so she could see what she would look like with a lower facelift.

"It will just give you a more refreshed look," he told her.

When she turned around, he moved closer to study her eyes, then he suggested that she consider having an upper eye blepharoplasty (an upper eye lift) procedure, too, so she would look "more awake."

As an afterthought, he recommended one more procedure.

"We can add some fat to your lips, too. . . . There wouldn't be any charge for that."

Until a few years ago, doctors made it a practice to only address the procedure(s) that a patient specifically asked about when they came in for a consultation, but that philosophy has changed in the last few years.

"We used to consider it inappropriate to mention other procedures; we don't want to sound like a salesman, but when we fix one thing, it calls attention to another," explained one surgeon.

"If a person has a facelift but doesn't have the bags under her eyes removed, she will not be happy with the results." Otherwise the skin will be tighter around their mouth, but the bags under the eyes will still be there and will be even more noticeable. It's better to point out the bags beforehand so the patient doesn't have unrealistic expectations about the facelift.

"It's like redecorating half a room. If you point out all the options that are available and what that will accomplish, then they can choose from the menu."

Altogether, the procedures for Dr. Tucker's potential client would be around $10,000, he told her, in spite of the fact that finances are usually handled by the office manager or a scheduling assistant—this practice lessens the risk of a misunderstanding that could be awkward to straighten out.

When the new client asked how long she would be in surgery for the recommended procedures, Dr. Tucker said that it would take about four hours, maybe a little longer, to perform the lower facelift and upper eye blepharo-plasty, and to sculpt her lips with filler.

There was no mention of the liposuction necessary to obtain the fat that would be used to fill her lips, which is considered a surgical procedure, since an incision would have to be made for a small rod to be inserted into the area to suction out the fat.

At that point the potential patient told Dr. Tucker that she was nervous about being under an anesthetic for four hours.

"It's all done under a local, there's just a mild anes-thetic to put you into a dreamy state, so you won't be aware of what is being done," he explained patiently.

"Sometimes people start to come out from under it [the anesthesia] . . . so if you just wiggle your toes, the nurse anesthetist will put you under again," he added, al-though it is the anesthesiologist's job to make sure the pa-tient stays within a sedation range and doesn't begin to come out from under the anesthesia.

After surgery he told the potential client she would rest in the recovery room in a recliner for a short time and then be moved to a bed.

"You'll stay overnight, someone will be here to watch over you," he added, although that was a departure from Sandra's after-surgery care. She was going to go home after a couple of hours in the recovery room.

He added that he performed surgery in the morning and then remained in the office from 1:30 p.m. until he went home around 7 p.m., so he would check in on her.

"I come in on Saturday, too, for post-surgery checkups."

Most of Dr. Tucker's long-term clients were aware that he had built a reputation on doing breast augmentations. "He's the plastic surgeon to the strippers," said one woman who has been going to Dr. Tucker for several years. Others who have continued seeing him since Sandra's death have declined to comment, even to say that they were pleased with his work.

"He has done seventy-five percent of the breast augmentation for the dancers in Charlotte," said plumber Rusty Alexander, who has known Dr. Tucker for years.

"When my ex-wife wanted to have some work, and our neighbor's wife wanted to do it at the same time, I took both of them to him. . . . He gave me a cut-rate for bringing him the business," Alexander recounted. Rusty's ex was delighted with Dr. Tucker's work, but Rusty hasn't been in touch with Peter Tucker since Sandra's death.

In an issue of *Supermodel* magazine in 2006, Dr. Tucker wrote a bylined article entitled "Breast Implants: Are They Right for You?" In it he talked about how Hollywood and the media have glorified larger breasts for some time. However, the newest trend was for a more proportioned look, he added.

He wrote about the many reasons for breast implants, suggesting that patients should have realistic expectations. He also explained the different types of implants, placement and possible complications that might occur.

He covered topics such as incisions, whether someone really needs a breast lift, mammograms before the surgery and what to expect the day of the procedure. The article was far more detailed than his in-office consultation.

"It is always possible to have a surgical complication, such as an infection," he said in the article. "There can also be permanent changes in the sensation in the breasts, or the implants," which he described as balloons, "which can break or rupture and will need to be replaced."

Tucker's website says he has performed thousands of facelifts with very satisfied clients. And the North Carolina Medical Board says there had never been any charges against Dr. Tucker until the malpractice suit in Sandra's death.

Dr. Tucker seems to have a laid-back style, rather unlike the rigid physicians most often seen. At one point, while talking to the potential new client about how minute the incisions would be in her hairline, he slipped off his surgical cap and pointed out a tiny scar in his own hairline, which, to the patient's surprise, had been made very recently when he'd had a brow lift.

On a light and playful note, the doctor related a cute story about a minister's wife who came to him for a consultation, accompanied by her husband.

"She asked if it was vain for her to want to find out about a facelift. Her husband, the minister, said, 'If a house needs painting, you paint it,'" Tucker recalled, laughing.

When asked about complications that might occur from the surgery the potential client was considering, Dr. Tucker mentioned two minor situations: a woman who had unexpected excessive bleeding after her surgery and another one who got an infection.

"We've been fortunate to only have one patient that developed an infection, and that was because she let her dog lick her on the face after her surgery," he explained.

The potential client was then escorted to the scheduler's office, where she was informed of tests that would need to be completed before the surgery. Finally they discussed the doctor's availability and methods of financing.

Ironically, a few months later, the local news carried a story about Dr. Tucker being stiffed. He had performed $10,000 worth of plastic surgery on two patients who had apparently scammed him out of the fee.

According to a police report, the patients had stolen someone's identity and used the financial information to have the procedures done. Dr. Tucker had no way of collecting the $10,000, nor did he respond to questions from the media about how he had been hoodwinked, which was not surprising. Dr. Tucker has never spoken publicly about Sandra Joyner's death, or of his nurse anesthetist being accused of murder, for that matter.

The day the potential client had her consultation with Dr. Tucker, his focus was clearly on the aesthetics of the surgery—how refreshed and wide-awake she would look after the procedures—not on the dangers or the possible side effects.

There was certainly no mention of the death of Sandra Joyner, or the upcoming murder trial of Sally Hill.

Dr. Tucker may have been the surgeon of choice for strippers who wanted breast augmentation, but his methods for drumming up new business when he first moved to Charlotte raised many an eyebrow in the medical community.

It didn't take long for word to get around that he was allegedly at strip clubs, handing out business cards wrapped in a $20 bills that he would supposedly put in the girls' G-strings, according to one local doctor. If true, it was a successful marketing tool, since he had a booming business for years with the reputation of "doctor to the strippers."

But locals and other doctors outside the Charlotte area thought such tactics a little too "out there." "On a moral and ethical basis, I have trouble with a doctor drumming up business in strip joints," said John O'Donnell, director of the nurse anesthetists at the University of Pittsburgh.

However, even his self-described forte didn't always produce the desired results. Occasionally other doctors ended up seeing his patients to straighten out problems that had occurred, instances where one breast was larger than the other or the scars were all too evident, for example.

If there were problems at times, Dr. Tucker would simply offer the patient her money back and suggest that she go someplace else to have the surgery redone.

"He wasn't a warm and fuzzy guy, he wasn't comforting when there was a problem," said one of Dr. Tucker's peers.

"Sometimes patients just cannot be satisfied," said a Chapel Hill plastic surgeon in Dr. Tucker's defense. "If someone has body dysmorphia"—an obsession with a particular body part like the nose or love handles—"many plastic surgeons are quick to suggest that the patient see a therapist before having surgery."

The problem isn't always something physical, he continued, but rather a misperception in the person's own mind. "Sometimes even after the patient sees a therapist, they will still want to have the surgery," he added.

If the surgeon suspects that someone has a distorted body image, he will likely refer the patient to someone else. "You can tell when someone won't ever be happy no matter what you do."

Most plastic surgeons learn to spot someone with body dysmorphia within five to ten minutes after they come into the office.

"Surprisingly we see body dysmorphia most often in a single, narcissistic male. You can never make them happy; you're stuck with them. I did three revisions on a man's nose job and he still wasn't happy. When I asked him what he wanted, he said he didn't know. Now, if I'm suspicious, I turn them down."

According to the Chapel Hill doctor, most plastic surgeons start out doing a lot of reconstruction because they see patients in the emergency room at hospitals. From there they begin to develop a reputation that brings in more plastic surgery patients.

He pointed out that the goals of aesthetic and cosmetic surgery are one and the same, usually to rejuvenate a person's face. Reconstructive surgery is performed to correct a congenital deformity such as a deformed skull or a cleft palate.

He also said that there are two different types of patients: those who want to look totally different, and want a makeover—smaller breasts and bigger hips, or vice versa—and those who just want to look the way they used to.

"Those will be around for years of maintenance," he adds of the latter.

Over the years, Sally had begun to notice what would bring people into the center for plastic surgery, as well. "In the beginning I enjoyed seeing most people feel better about themselves, but then I began to realize that some of them would benefit more from counseling instead of plastic surgery," she said.

After her death, Dr. Tucker made it clear to everyone that he was not responsible for what had happened to Sandra. He pointed out that even the medical board had said Sally's actions were, to some degree, beyond his control. He would take every opportunity to tell his peers that her death was not his fault, even when it was merely thought to have been accidental. He'd professed his innocence about any wrongdoing all along, complaining from the onset that there should be a criminal investigation. Instead there was a medical board investigation that focused on his shortfalls in supervising Sally Hill, and the lack of proper procedures, especially in case of an emergency. He could have lost his license because of it, but instead, the North Carolina Medical Board only suspended his license for twelve months and then stayed that suspension so long as Dr. Tucker agreed to implement better procedures for closer supervision of his nurse anesthetist and to begin monitoring those procedures.

Before Dr. Tucker's deposition to the medical board

was sealed, *The Charlotte Observer* reported that Tucker had said that on the day of Sandra's death Sally Hill was out of control, she was not herself that day. He claimed she was "grossly negligent" and said he believed that there had been an element of malicious behavior involved in Sandra's death. The medical board ultimately agreed with Dr. Tucker that Sally's actions were grossly negligent and that Dr. Tucker could not be held responsible for Sally's gross negligence.

Some believe that Dr. Tucker was the anonymous person who later provided the district attorney with information that led to the reopening of the case as a homicide early in 2007. However, whatever that person's identity, it has never been officially revealed.

The medical board disciplined Dr. Tucker for failing to supervise Sally Hill, but "they stopped short of laying the death at Dr. Tucker's feet," according to Thomas Mansfield, head of the board's legal department.

The structuring of the North Carolina Medical Board may also have helped Tucker avoid more serious charges because seven of the twelve members of the medical board are appointed by the North Carolina Medical Society, a powerful private special interest group with 11,000 members statewide. In recent years, various attempts by legislators to rein in the medical society's power over the board, through bills that end its ability to appoint its members, have gone down in flames because of the society's proficient lobbyists.

After looking into Dr. Tucker's role in Sandra Joyner's death, the medical board allowed him to continue to practice in exchange for his agreeing to do a better job managing his nurses and allowing the board to inspect his office at any time.

In the end, it said the board was "fully confident and satisfied" that it was safe for Tucker to practice medicine.

Even so, Dr. Tucker's career and life were seriously impacted by Sandra Joyner's death in his office. "He was like a whipped puppy for about a year and a half," a peer recalled at the time.

In the aftermath of Dr. Tucker's hearing, his malpractice carrier dropped him, although this is not unusual after a major case of this kind. He told his peers that he had to go offshore to get a company to insure him, and even then he was required to pay exorbitant premiums. None of this was surprising considering Sandra's death, although it was not because of his surgery.

As one of his peers pointed out, Dr. Tucker still had some liability for Sandra's death. They agree that the person in charge [the doctor] is ultimately responsible for what happens in the office.

TEN

After Sandra's Death

Sally was devastated. She couldn't have been more distraught when Sandra died, according to family and friends.

"It's all my fault," she had told her co-workers and those closest to her, people who had known her for years.

"She talked about it a lot when it first happened," explained Patty Campbell, who'd worked at the Center for Cosmetic and Plastic Surgery for years until sometime before Sandra's death. "She felt awful about it."

Patty believed Sally's grief was a normal reaction. "She was really upset that Sandra had died. I wasn't in the recovery room, I don't know what happened. Sally probably thought she could handle it when Sandra went into respiratory arrest."

Patty explained that Sally "was probably in shock" as she just stood there instead of trying to resuscitate the patient.

When Sally's earlier comment—"She's the one who stole my boyfriend in high school," made during Sandra's 1999 visit to the office—came to light, investigators questioned Patty about it.

"I didn't hear the comment, but I know Sally," Patty said later. "I know she wouldn't hold a grudge for thirty years. She didn't do it," she said emphatically. "If she were that upset [about the boyfriend], she would have done something about it long before. She would have poisoned her at the twenty-fifth high school reunion or gotten a gun and shot her," she said, tongue-in-cheek. "The police are making too much of the remark. We all say stupid things. She is wrongly accused. She doesn't have a mean bone in her body."

Patty knew Sally fairly well outside of the office.

"Sally talked about Sandra's death, she talked about her marriage, her parents; she never once mentioned anything that happened in high school. Sally is a devout Christian. When Sandra died, she said if it weren't for her faith she wouldn't be able to deal with it," Patty recalled. "I'm sure she would give her life not to have this happen to a patient," she added. "I know Sally didn't do this, I would trust her with my life."

Other nurses Sally has worked with have said the same thing.

"She was always good at her job, we all trusted her," said a former co-worker.

And those who knew Sally and Sandra thirty years ago found it impossible to comprehend how this might have even happened.

"It was a huge shocker," said Pam Sargent, who was Sally's best friend in high school, though they had lost touch after they graduated. "I just couldn't get it through my mind. It's so ridiculous to me to think that she would hold a grudge for thirty years."

A family member said, "This is unfathomable that Sally would be accused of murdering Sandra. It makes no sense. It's a bunch of hooey."

Even more surprising, since the police have indicated that Sally intentionally gave Sandra too much pain medication over a thirty-year grudge about a boyfriend, is that Sally has said, "I don't even know what boyfriend the police are referring to." She admits knowing Sandra then, but only as an acquaintance.

"I didn't really know Sandra that well in high school. When I was in the ninth grade, they asked me to be a cheerleader; Sandra was on the panel.

"I wanted to be a cheerleader so bad, and she helped them pick me because she was one of the judges," added Sally, who was an alternate letter girl and part of the flag corps at Olympic High.

"I always admired her, I thought she was really nice," Sally continued.

Saying again that she does not know what boyfriend police are referring to, Sally said that Sandra "was already with her future husband when we were in high school. Besides, I never had any trouble getting a boyfriend."

Friends who have known Sally for much of her adult life are sure Sally did nothing to intentionally harm Sandra.

"There is just no way you would ever think of her doing something like this," said a former co-worker.

Still it's hard to understand how so many things could have gone so wrong that day—the alarm that was turned off on the pulse oximeter, Sally being out of the room when her patient's blood pressure and oxygen levels had dropped way too low. Especially puzzling was Sally's lackadaisical attitude when Sandra was clearly in trouble.

In his deposition in 2003, Dr. Tucker said Sally was not herself on the day of Sandra's death. In fact, he'd said, "she's flipped out. She's going nuts. She snapped."

Sally's medical files are not public record because of the Health Insurance Portability & Accountability Act (HIPAA) guidelines, but some have wondered if something other than jealousy could have caused Sally's seeming insensitivity to Sandra's complications that day.

Could it be that she was experiencing negative effects of cancer treatment?

Sally had undergone chemotherapy for leukemia before Sandra's second surgery, which no doubt had some lasting effects, such as fatigue and lethargy.

Most people—70–90 percent—who have had chemotherapy vividly recall the chronic fatigue that affected them physically, mentally and spiritually for up to a year after the treatment. Everyday life was hard work, and there was a long period of time when they could barely get through the day.

The website Cancerhelp.org has reported that chemotherapy patients may feel like "I just cannot be bothered to do much." They don't sleep well and feel it is hard to get up in the morning. They feel anxious and depressed, and have muscle pain. Patients often find themselves breathless after doing the smallest tasks, like taking a shower or making the bed. It is hard to concentrate when watching TV or talking to a good friend. It is also hard to make clear decisions.

Another major side effect that many reported is memory loss—a feeling of being "fuzzy," "cloudy" or "in a fog."

In April 2007, *The New York Times* published an article entitled " 'Chemo Brain': Not in Patients' Heads." In it Jane Gross mentioned an Internet website filled with comments from people who were suffering from the effects of chemotherapy and the mental fog that comes with it. A good many who made comments did so with humor to take the edge off of a frightening condition.

One woman found five unopened gallons of milk in the refrigerator, with no memory of the first four she had purchased. Another asked her husband which toothbrush was hers. A third reported filling the glasses at the Thanksgiving table with gravy instead of water.

At first these symptoms were not given much stock. But lately attitudes have been changing.

"Until recently oncologists would discount it, trivialize it, make patients feel it was all in their heads," said Dr. Daniel Silverman, a cancer researcher at the University of California, Los Angeles, who studies the cognitive effects of chemotherapy. "Now there's enough literature, even if it's controversial, to indicate that not mentioning it as a possibility is either ignorant or an evasion of professional duty," he continued.

" 'Chemo brain' is part of the language now, and just to have it acknowledged makes a difference," claimed Anne Grant, who owns a picture-framing business in New York and who had high-dose chemotherapy and a bone marrow transplant in 1995. She could not concentrate well enough to read, she garbled her sentences and struggled with simple decisions like which socks to wear.

Virtually all cancer survivors who have had toxic treatments like chemotherapy experience short-term memory loss and difficulty concentrating during and shortly afterwards, experts say. But a vast majority improve.

About 15 percent, or roughly 360,000 of the nation's 2.4 million female breast cancer survivors—the group that has dominated research on cognitive side effects—said that they remained distracted years later, according to some of the experts. Yet nobody knows what distinguishes this 15 percent.

Clues come from studies too small to be considered definitive. One such study found a gene linked to Alzheimer's disease in cancer survivors with cognitive deficits. Another, using PET scans that monitor organ function, found unusual activity in the part of the brain that controls short-term recall.

The central puzzle of chemo brain is that many of the symptoms associated with the treatment can occur for

other, unrelated reasons. Could there have been another
reason for Sally's odd behavior?

At the time of Sandra Joyner's death there was no investigation into Sally Hill, or Dr. Tucker for that matter. Because it was determined that Sandra's death had been
caused by a medical error, it was ruled an accident.

Had there been a thorough investigation at the time,
another reason for Sally's strange reaction in an emergency situation might have been found.

In a five-page memo dated October 26, 2006, Assistant
District Attorney Elizabeth "Beth" Freeman asked for disclosure relating to witnesses, searches and any evidence
that had been found in regard to the murder charges against
Sally.

In the memo there was a request involving drug activity
which asked for "Any information from law enforcement
and/or school or business officials concerning the defendant's lack of reputation for dealing drugs or receiving or
possessing stolen property in the school, place of business
or other location." The next item referenced "Any information tending to show the defendant participated merely
as a conduit for other parties in any alleged drug sale or
other illegal activity."

The possibility of drug abuse has never specifically
been mentioned, and when Detective Chuck Henson was
asked about the comments in Beth Freeman's request for
disclosure, he said the mention of drugs was standard.
The possibility that Sally might have been taking the pain
medications that were often missing in the office was
dismissed by Henson, though the prosecution certainly
would not tip its hand if that were going to come up at
trial.

However, there are plenty of statistics to prove that it is
not uncommon for nurses (and doctors) to become addicted

to pain medication because the narcotics are so readily available in the workplace.

According to the American Nurses Association one in twelve nurses in the U.S. has an alcohol or drug problem severe enough to affect his or her practice. Listed among the top signs to watch for are the disappearance of drugs and medication logs that have been changed. In Sally's case, several doses of fentanyl turned up missing, and her medication audit forms show the log had been changed eleven out of forty-three times. In one case the wrong date was given—it should have been the day before that the drugs were taken.

In fact, if proper procedures had been followed, narcotics were supposed to be kept under lock and key, signed out only with another person present and entered into the log immediately. If drugs were to be disposed of, someone was to witness that as well.

If Sally was under the influence, it certainly wouldn't be the first time a medical professional's response was impaired by something other than incompetence, as some have suggested was the case when Sandra died.

"Fentanyl is the drug of choice among anesthetic personnel under the age of forty; for those over forty, it is alcohol," said Barry Friedberg, well-respected anesthetist who practices in Coronado, California. "It is not like Demerol. It's sneaky, you can squirt it in your morning coffee or a can of soda." More significant, he explained that when a urine screen is performed, the fentanyl cannot be detected if the person has taken a Valium by mouth. Fentanyl also comes in skin patches and lollipops for children.

"The scope of the problem is big," Elizabeth Moran Fitzgerald, ARNP, LMFT, Ed.D., has said.

John O'Donnell estimates that the numbers for nurse anesthetists are higher than for nurses, more like 10 to 20 percent, as are the statistics for doctors.

Opiates such as Demerol, morphine, and Vicodin, a brand of hydrocodone, are the most often used drugs. "Fentanyl is a common choice of drug because it goes away really fast," O'Donnell explained.

Addiction specialists point out that job stress is often the cause of a medical professional's use of drugs or alcohol. "Nurses are under terrific stress right now—more work, higher patient load, less help," Dr. James Lea, of the Hazelden rehab center, has said. "I think that's awfully stressful. The stress of being asked to do more than they feel they can do safely is real common."

It is also common to use narcotics for pain relief, which often leads to addiction or self-medicating for depression.

"Nobody starts out to be, or feels they would ever become, addicted," Lea added. "But it's a terrible problem, mostly because of patient care issues."

Several websites list behaviors that might indicate a nurse could be addicted. Among the signs to watch for:

— Arriving early, staying late and coming to work on unscheduled days off.
— Excessively wasting drugs.
— Regularly signing out large quantities of controlled drugs.
— Often volunteering to give medication to other nurses' patients.
— Taking frequent bathroom breaks.
— Patients reporting unrelieved pain despite an adequate prescription of pain medication.
— Discrepancies in the documentation of controlled substances.
— Medications being signed out for patients who have been discharged or transferred, or who are off the unit for procedures or tests.

Suzanne Durburg, executive director of the Illinois Organization of Nurse Leaders, says, "Usually there is a problem on the unit with unaccounted loss of narcotics. That's probably the most prevalent sign."

If the nurse gets her drugs at the hospital, he added, "What I've discovered is that some of these nurses are people who have perhaps the best reputation of caregiver on the unit, and people are shocked when they discover a nurse is impaired."

"I see the problem of nurse addiction to be a particularly difficult one because their access is so profound," added Lea. "The doctor may order the controlled substances, but the nurse is the one who has it in her hot little hands."

Another big sign of trouble is a nurse who claims she disposed of a drug "because it would be wasted anyway," or when the nurse begins to get sloppy about covering up her addiction, explained Lea.

Barbara Vieu, RN, CD and Hazelden Springbrook's manager of health services, said part of the problem is that drugs are available and accessible, making them easy to abuse. "It's very important for health professionals to understand that they have the same problem as anyone else—maybe higher quality drugs and more sterile techniques, but the disease is exactly the same," Lea added.

But even with missing drugs and erratic behavior, Sally has not been charged with any drug use. In fact, the prosecution has alleged that the extra five ccs of fentanyl that was found to be missing after Sandra's death might have been given to Sandra in addition to the seven ccs that were on the record.

ELEVEN

Legal and Medical Action

Not surprisingly, in 2003, before the two-year grace period was up, John Joyner filed a malpractice suit against Dr. Tucker, Sally Hill and the Center for Plastic and Cosmetic Surgery on behalf of the estate of Sandra Joyner.

The legal action was overseen by G. Miller Jordan (not related to Sally) because of a rift between John and Sandra's family.

Mark Holt of Kirby & Holt in Raleigh, North Carolina, represented John Joyner, and Charlotte attorney John Golding represented Sally Hill. Neither lawyer has ever publicly commented on the outcome. A year later the suit was settled out of court and the terms have remained confidential; however, the settlement was rumored to have been several million.

According to the American Society of Plastic Surgeons (ASPS), in 2004, a study showed that deaths occurring at office-based surgery facilities are rare, less than one-quarter percent. From 2000 to 2002, serious complications were infrequent, only 1 in 298 cases or 0.34 percent, with death occurring at 1 in 51,459 cases. The study said that number was comparable to the overall risk of such procedures performed in hospital surgeries.

In North Carolina there are 255 licensed plastic surgeons, in South Carolina 91. The North Carolina Medical Board estimates that there are 1,000 complaints (all specialties) annually; South Carolina averages forty to fifty a year, all specialties. The board has just announced a plan to begin listing all complaints against doctors on its website, something physicians are lobbying against.

According to the medical board's website, in 2006 there were sixty-six suspensions involving fifty-five physicians, eight physician assistants and three nurse practitioners. In that same year there were twenty-nine suspensions of physicians, physician assistants and nurse practitioners in South Carolina.

In 2005 the numbers were slightly lower: forty-six suspensions (physicians and physician assistants); sixteen medical professionals surrendered their licenses (including three physicians and three physician assistants).

When the medical board has determined that a formal action should be taken, the practitioner is offered the option of signing an agreement (a consent order) to address the problem. Consent orders most often require changes in practice or behavior, and place conditions or limitations on the practice.

If the board does not believe the physician is an imminent risk to the public, it may hold a hearing before a full board, a panel of the board or an administrative law judge. The hearings are open to the public, and charges, consent orders and other board action documents are public and available on the medical board's website.

The principal grounds for action by the board include unprofessional, immoral or dishonorable conduct; professional incompetence or failure to maintain professional standards; being unable to practice medicine with skill and safety due to illness, drug or alcohol use, or physical or mental abnormality; conviction of a felony, a crime involving the practice of medicine or a crime involving moral turpitude; or producing or attempting to produce an abortion contrary to law.

Other grounds include: obtaining or attempting to obtain something of value by false representations; professing to treat a patient under a system or school of treatment or practice other than that for which they are educated; promoting the sale of drugs or other items, or attempting to exploit a patient; and making false statements or representations to the board, or failure to respond to the board or disciplinary action by another licensing jurisdiction.

Despite the low death rate in office-based surgery facilities, even less invasive procedures can sometimes lead to complications and fatalities.

In 2007, a North Carolina State University senior died from a reaction to numbing cream applied before her laser hair removal. The North Carolina Medical Board held a hearing on the case involving a Cary, North Carolina, doctor Samuel Wurster, who was affiliated with a clinic. Wurster was reprimanded and has not renewed his license.

In 2005 the North Carolina Medical Board reprimanded doctors at Southeastern Plastic Surgery for distributing inaccurate marketing materials on a Botox-like wrinkle drug. The drug literature claimed it was "proven safe in clinical trials." Months later doctors became aware through mainstream media that the FDA was investigating the manufacturers of the product they were using, according to medical board reports. The doctors immediately notified all patients who had received the product, none of whom had been harmed.

Although the North Carolina Medical Board acknowledges thousands of complaints a year, Thomas Mansfield, attorney for the board, pointed out that, "Dr. Tucker is the only one who has ever been publicly disciplined."

Right after the malpractice suit, the medical board launched an investigation into Dr. Tucker as a result of

Sandra's death. A seven-page document filed by the North Carolina Medical Board on May 1, 2003, listed several charges and allegations against Tucker, who had been licensed to practice medicine and perform surgery since May 2, 1987.

Ultimately the board found that Dr. Tucker had, in fact, provided substandard care in several areas of practice on the day of Sandra's death:

- He had admitted the patient to the recovery room without providing written orders regarding the patients' post-operative care.

- In the recovery room the patient had received an injection of 2 ccs of a fentanyl citrate IV from Dr. Tucker's nurse anesthetist, which caused the patient to suffer respiratory depression and arrest, making resuscitative measures necessary.

- After taking resuscitative measures, the medical staff had failed to recognize that the patient was still suffering from symptoms consistent with profound respiratory depression.

- His staff had failed to intubate and ventilate the patient as part of their resuscitative measures.

The medical board's investigation also found that:

- Dr. Tucker and his staff's failures had directly led to the patient's death.

- He had allowed the patient to be admitted and treated in his recovery room without specific postoperative orders written and signed by himself.

- He had failed to supervise his nurse anesthetist sufficiently, and his lack of adequate supervision contributed to the administration of 2 ccs of fentanyl in the recovery room without a written or verbal order from Dr. Tucker. There was also no documentation in the patient's medical record as to who had ordered the fentanyl.

The findings stated that his failure to supervise the nurse anesthetist had also contributed to the choice and administration of fentanyl as a post-operative pain medication.

It was determined to be below the standard of practice in North Carolina for 2 ccs of fentanyl to be used as a post-operative pain medication under the facts and circumstances that had been presented in the care of the patient.

Dr. Tucker's failure to supervise his staff sufficiently had contributed to failure to intubate and ventilate the patient as part of the resuscitative measures, and to the staff considering the patient stable after their initial attempts at resuscitation when the patient's oxygen saturation count had decreased to 81. The board went on to say that a count of 81 still indicated profound respiratory depression and meant that the patient should have been intubated and ventilated.

Clearly, this condition had contributed to Sandra's death, they said.

They also included several other procedures that were deemed to be not up to par.

Dr. Tucker had failed to perform several pre-operative laboratory procedures including a full blood panel, urinalysis and EKG. A review of the record indicated that Dr. Tucker had only performed a hemoglobin test for the patient as part of a pre-operative lab workup.

He had also administered four milligrams of Zofran and 10 milligrams of Valium to the patient, apparently without a written or verbal consent from Sandra or her physican, since there was no record of it in her file.

The record mentioned "lip infiltrate 850c" to be used in plumping up her lips, but did not state what the infiltrate was, i.e., water, saline, along with lidocaine and epinephrine that was mixed with the patient's body fat. There was a note and consent form for the patient's fat to be used to increase the upper and lower lips; however, the note does not state how the fat was obtained, nor by what technique it was placed in the patient's lips.

In addition Dr. Tucker's pre-operative history and physical of the patient had not been signed or dated.

However, the report acknowledged that these substandard procedures did not contribute to the patient's death.

On November 20, 2003, the medical board advised Dr. Tucker that the charges and allegations, which constituted unprofessional conduct, entitled the board to suspend, revoke or limit his license to practice medicine and perform surgery, or it could deny any application he might make in the future, such as adding new procedures to his practice.

A hearing on the charges was set up for later that month. Dr. Tucker had the option to appear personally and, through counsel, was entitled to cross-examine witnesses and present evidence in his behalf. Or he could file his responses to the charges with the board within thirty days. At that point the name of the patient and where the surgery took place had not been made public and would remain withheld until the matter was settled.

Then the board turned its attention to Sally Hill. The North Carolina Medical Board found that she had been "grossly negligent" in her care and treatment of Sandra Joyner on April 10, 2001, because she had not notified Dr. Tucker about Sandra's worsening condition.

They also said she'd performed "medical acts" without authorization.

According to the medical board:

— She had failed to adequately and appropriately assess the physical history and the condition of Sandra prior to surgery.

— She had failed to provide a safe environment for her patient in the course of surgical treatment and post-operative periods.

— She had failed to perform assessments in the post-operative period.

— She had failed to monitor and document her patient's condition in the post-operative period.

— She had failed to monitor and document Sandra's response to narcotic pain medication.

— She had failed to respond to a patient in respiratory distress and arrest.

— She had failed to document the medical care and treatment when Sandra suffered respiratory distress and arrest.

— She had failed to establish and maintain airways in a patient with respiratory distress and arrest.

— She had failed to summon emergency medical assistance in a timely manner.

— She had failed to comply with standards of practice among CRNAs with similar training and experience in the same or similar communities.

— She had failed to use her best judgment, and to exercise reasonable care and diligence in her care and treatment of Sandra.

— She had failed to possess the degree of learning, skill and ability that other similarly situated professionals ordinarily possess.

— She had failed to exercise reasonable care and diligence in the application of her knowledge and skill.

TWELVE

Safe Surgery

Of course every patient believes they will have a safe, uneventful surgery, trusting that the medical professionals they have chosen will have their best interests in mind.

The American Society of Plastic Surgeons (ASPS), which estimates that there are 17,000 plastic surgeons in business, about 90 percent of them board-certified, has stated that plastic surgery patients should remember that "the decision to have a plastic surgery procedure is serious. No-risk surgery does not exist!"

The organization has recommended six guidelines for anyone who is considering a plastic surgery or cosmetic procedure:

1. Do your homework: Research the procedure, the benefits and the risks. Go to http://www.plasticsurgery.org for the latest information on plastic surgery procedures.

2. Have realistic expectations: Ask your plastic surgeon about the benefits and risks of your surgery; discuss your expectations and understand side effects and recovery time.

3. Be informed: Talk to patients who have had your procedure so you know what to expect.

4. Ask tough questions: Consult with your plastic surgeon and discuss your full medical history to determine the most appropriate treatment.

5. Choose an ASPS Member Surgeon: ASPS Member Surgeons are qualified, trained and properly certified. They adhere to a strict code of ethics, receive continuous education and operate only in accredited facilities.

6. Confirm the accreditation of the outpatient surgery center: If your surgery may take place in an outpatient surgery center, be sure it is accredited. ASPS requires that all members who perform surgery under anesthesia must do so in a facility that meets certain criteria, such as the appropriate accreditation and state licensure.

"It's one thing to have training, but it's another to have your competency tested. This is why board-certification by The American Board of Plastic Surgery [ABPS] is so crucial," said Dr. Richard D'Amico. "As a patient, you should ask yourself, 'Why wouldn't this surgeon be board-certified in plastic surgery?'"

A prospective patient can rest assured that all ABPS-certified physicians have:

- Graduated from an accredited medical school;

- Completed at least five years of surgical residency training, usually three years of general surgery and two years of plastic surgery;

• Practiced plastic surgery for two years; and

• Passed comprehensive written and oral examinations covering both the cosmetic and reconstructive areas of the specialty of plastic surgery.

According to medical records, both Dr. Tucker and Sally Hill were current with all their licenses and board certifications at the time of Sandra's death.

But even at the highest level of care, every surgery has risks as well as benefits. The ASPS recognizes that the physician–patient relationship is one of shared decision-making. It is called informed consent.

The ASPS "Statement of Principle on Informed Consent" details the information that should be discussed and understood by the patient, including: details of the surgery; benefits, possible consequences and side effects of the operation; potential risks and adverse outcomes as well as their probability and severity; alternatives to the procedure being considered and their benefits, risks and consequences; and the anticipated outcome.

The ASPS has said plastic surgery is consistently reliable and generally considered safe. While complications are rare, there are still risks and complications, just like any other surgical procedure. The organization stresses the importance of blood tests and a physical before surgery. Some of the general risks associated with the procedures may include bleeding in the first twenty-four hours and hematomas that form when the blood pools and collects under the skin.

The organization points out that within the first twenty-four hours, a patient is more susceptible to secondary infection, since bacterial and viral pathogens have easier access via open wounds, sutures, or drain sites. That is why antibiotics are usually given during and following the procedures. Any fever, redness in a local area, foul odor and/or thick yellow or white discharge should be reported immediately.

Seromas are similar to hematomas, except a seroma is a collection of tissue fluid rather than blood, and they often occur after tummy tucks. They can be recognized by enlargement, heaviness, and even sloshing of fluid and are treated with compression or drainage with a needle or syringe.

Another risk is sutures, which the immune system sometimes reacts to. The body can produce scar tissue as the suture tries to separate from the body, causing a bump under the skin. A suture abscess is indicated by redness, tenderness and pus around the closure. Sometimes the surgeon will have to re-suture or correct the scar when it heals.

Occasionally there will be necrosis, the death of tissues, which is generally caused by insufficient oxygen to the affected areas. The risk is minimal, but sometimes does occur with facelifts, tummy tucks and breast reductions when flaps are created to separate the skin and its blood supply from underlying structures. There will be a gray cast to the skin and the patient will have corresponding pain.

Sometimes nerve damage can occur simply from the injection of anesthesia. The patient will notice numbness, tingling or a change in sensation. Weakness or paralysis to the affected muscles may last up to six months.

The organization is careful to point out that adverse reactions to anesthesia are generally rare, but nevertheless complications can occur. Nausea is common, as is sore throat associated with a breathing tube, but generally only lasts a day or so.

In very rare cases, adverse reactions can become serious such as documented cases of seizures, heart attacks and high temperatures that might lead to death. But overall, most people do not suffer any complications, the organization points out.

Scarring is one of the most common risks patients should be aware of. During the process of healing, visible thickening of the skin edges and new red bumps called granulation tissue form in and around the shrinking wound and often result in a scar. They will usually diminish within a short time.

Most surgeons try to hide incision lines in places where they aren't noticeable, like under the crease of the breast in breast augmentation surgery or beneath the swimwear line in a tummy tuck.

The organization points out that nerve damage can be a serious complication. Some people who undergo plastic surgery lose feeling in the area that was operated on, while others may experience problems moving muscles where the surgery was performed.

Anesthesia and sedation have their own set of possible complications, among them abnormal heart rhythms, airway obstructions, blood clots, heart attack, malignant hyperthermia, nerve damage, stroke and temporary paralysis.

Of course the most serious is brain damage and subsequent death if there is a serious lack of oxygen to the brain over a period of minutes. Brain damage can occur if blood circulation becomes depressed at dangerous levels.

Obstructions sometimes irritate air passages, causing the vocal cords to spasm and block the airway. At that point the anesthesiologist may need to insert a tube down the throat or cut into the windpipe to allow the patient to breathe.

Malignant hyperthermia is a rare complication when body temperature, blood pressure and heart rate all rise to hyperactive levels. If not treated quickly the condition can lead to death.

Blood clots in the veins can also be fatal. Longer operating times and general anesthesia increase the risk of deep vein thrombosis (DVT).

A drop in blood pressure can be normal during surgery. However, a sudden drop due to blood loss could lead to irregular heartbeat and possibly a heart attack.

The risk of infection is less than one percent, and antibiotics reduce that risk dramatically. However, if it does occur, it can be very serious.

It is generally known that patients with heart trouble, lung disease or obesity are at greater risk of complications from anesthesia. It is important for the patient to discuss his or her medical history and to tell the doctor about any medications that they are taking.

Sometimes aspiration can occur if the patient vomits during surgery and the liquid is forced into the lungs. It can cause mild discomfort and lead to infections and obstruction in the lungs, and occasionally pneumonia.

Excessive bleeding can also create major complications. If it occurs in surgery, the doctor and anesthesiologist should recognize it by pooling blood or by a drop in blood pressure.

The American Society for Aesthetic Plastic Surgery (ASAPS) has reported that in a 1997 survey based on more than 400,000 operations performed in accredited facilities, less than half of one percent had serious complications. Additionally, the mortality rate was extremely low—only one in 57,000 cases.

Dr. Rod Rohrich, president of the American Society of Plastic Surgeons says, "In America, it's amazing, most women spend more time finding a pair of shoes than they do finding a cosmetic surgeon. You can take the shoes back, you can't take your face back or your life back."

THIRTEEN

Guidelines

The American Association of Plastic Surgeons has specific guidelines that should be followed to ensure a patient's safety as well.

- The facility should have a medical director or governing body that establishes policy and is responsible for the activities of the facility and its staff. It is their responsibility to ensure that the facilities and personnel are adequate and appropriate for the type of procedures performed.

- The policies and procedures should be in writing for the orderly conduct of the facility and reviewed on an annual basis.

- The medical director or governing body should ensure that all applicable local, state and federal regulations are observed.

- All health care practitioners and nurses should hold a valid license or certificate to perform their assigned duties.

- All operating room personnel who provide clinical care in the office should be qualified to perform services commensurate with appropriate levels of education, training and experience.

- The anesthesiologist should participate in ongoing continuous quality improvement and risk management activities.

- The medical director or governing body should recognize the basic human rights of its patients, and a written document that describes this policy should be available for patients to review.

In regard to the safety in the facility, the office should:

- Comply with all applicable federal, state and local laws, codes and regulations pertaining to fire prevention, building construction and occupancy, accommodations for the disabled, occupational safety and health, and disposal of medical waste and hazardous waste.

- Policies and procedures should comply with laws and regulations pertaining to controlled drug supply, storage and administration.

In regard to care of the patient, it is pertinent that:

- The anesthesiologist should be satisfied that the procedure to be undertaken is within the scope of practice of the health care practitioners and the capabilities of the facility.

- The procedure should be of a duration and degree of complexity that will permit the patient to recover and be discharged from the facility.

- Patients who by reason of preexisting medical or other conditions may be at undue risk for complications should be referred to an appropriate facility for performance of the procedure and the administration of anesthesia.

Once the surgery is completed:

- The anesthesiologist should adhere to the "Basic Standards for Preanesthesia Care," "Standards for Basic Anesthetic Monitoring," "Standards for Postanesthesia Care" and "Guidelines for Ambulatory Anesthesia and Surgery" as currently promulgated by the American Society of Anesthesiologists.

- The anesthesiologist should be physically present during the intraoperative period and immediately available until the patient has been discharged from anesthesia care.

- Discharge of the patient is a physician responsibility. This decision should be documented in the medical record.

- Personnel with training in advanced resuscitative techniques (e.g., ACLS, PALS) should be immediately available until all patients are discharged home.

Other guidelines that involve safety include:

- At a minimum, all facilities should have a reliable source of oxygen, suction, resuscitation equipment and emergency drugs. Specific reference is made to the ASA "Guidelines for Nonoperating Room Anesthetizing Locations."

- There should be sufficient space to accommodate all necessary equipment and personnel and to allow for expeditious access to the patient, anesthesia machine (when present) and all monitoring equipment.

- All equipment should be maintained, tested and inspected according to the manufacturer's specifications.

- Back-up power sufficient to ensure patient protection in the event of an emergency should be available.

- In any location in which anesthesia is administered, there should be appropriate anesthesia apparatus and equipment which allow monitoring consistent with ASA "Standards for Basic Anesthetic Monitoring" and documentation of regular preventive maintenance as recommended by the manufacturer.

- In an office where anesthesia services are to be provided to infants and children, the required equipment, medication and resuscitative capabilities should be appropriately sized for a pediatric population.

In case of an emergency:

- All facility personnel should be appropriately trained in and regularly review the facility's written emergency protocols.

- There should be written protocols for cardiopulmonary emergencies and other internal and external disasters such as fire.

- The facility should have medications, equipment and written protocols available to treat malignant hyperthermia when triggering agents are used.

- The facility should have a written protocol in place for the safe and timely transfer of patients to a pre-specified alternate care facility when extended or emergency services are needed to protect the health or well-being of the patient.

According to the subsequent finding of the Nursing Board, it would seem that many of Sally's infractions fell short of these guidelines.

As early as the mid-1950s doctors and hospitals began to look into the status of anesthesia patient safety. "A Study of the Deaths Associated with Anesthesia and Surgery," which appeared in the *Annals of Surgery* strongly suggested an inherent toxicity in the neuromuscular blocking drugs (according to information provided by the Anesthesia Patient Safety Foundation (APSF).

The publication was one of the first to consider anesthesia deaths. Over a five-year period nearly 600,000 anesthetics administered in ten universities were studied. It noted who the anesthetists were, what techniques and agents were used and whether the trachea was intubated. The incidence of mortality was found to be 3.7 per

10,000 anesthetics, with anesthesia as a primary cause.

A year later several anesthesiologists published a paper saying they "believed that many of the important conclusions drawn were not justified on the basis of the statistics presented."

A few years later the University of Pennsylvania reviewed 33,000 patients given either a general anesthetic to which neuromuscular blockers were added or a spinal anesthetic. There were no deaths attributable to anesthesia, although the overall mortality rate with anesthesia as the primary cause was 11.7 per 10,000 anesthetics.

Then in 1959 a study found anesthesia to be the principal cause of mortality in some 6 percent of the deaths and a contributing factor in 13 percent. At that point death by anesthesia, which had not been previously analyzed, was declared a major public health problem, which caused increased interest among anesthetists in improving anesthesia outcomes.

Then in 1984 a large teaching hospital conducted forty-seven interviews of staff and resident anesthesiologists. In the end 1,089 descriptions of preventable critical incidents were collected and the following corrective strategies were recommended.

— Train, educate and supervise.
— Use appropriate monitoring instrumentation and vigilance.
— Recognize the limitations influencing individual performance.
— Establish and follow preparation and inspection protocol.
— Assure equipment performance.
— Design and organize work space.
— Act on incident reports.
— Eliminate pitfalls.

FOURTEEN

Nursing Board

Shortly after the medical board found that Dr. Tucker had failed to adequately supervise Sally, that he allowed sloppy practice of office procedures and especially the fact that there were no written orders for post-operative care or emergency procedures, the North Carolina Board of Nursing launched its own investigation into Sally Hill's actions on that fateful day.

In a letter to Sally dated September 2, 2004, the board said, "You were involved in an incident that indicates you may not be safe and competent to practice nursing or that you may have violated the Nursing Practice Act."

Specifically the medical board investigation had shown that she'd failed to maintain an accurate record regarding patient care and to report information crucial to the safety of a patient.

Sally had provided contract anesthesia services for Dr. Tucker's office since 1997. She usually worked Wednesday, Thursday, and Friday, then Monday and Tuesday one week, then she would be off for a week. In the capacity of Certified Registered Nurse Anesthetist, Sally was responsible for the patient during the pre-surgical interview and induction, throughout the surgical procedure and until the

Sandra Baker, a junior in 1972.

Olympic High School yearbook, 1972

Sally Jordan, a sophomore in 1972.

Olympic High School yearbook, 1972

Olympic High School in 2008.

John Franklin Joyner, a senior in 1972.

Olympic High School yearbook, 1972

John on the wrestling team.

Olympic High School yearbook, 1973

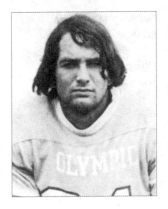

James Niell, the "boyfriend" in question.

Photo courtesy of James Niell

Olympic High School Coach Joe White, who knew all the kids well.

Olympic High School yearbook, 1973

Sandra was the head of the cheerleading squad.

Olympic High School yearbook, 1972

Sandra joking around after school.

Olympic High School yearbook, 1972

Pam Sargent, Sally's best friend in 1972.

Olympic High School yearbook, 1972

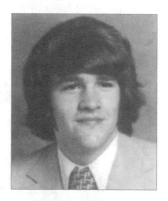

Gregg Pence in 1972, who reconnected with Sandra after her separation.

Olympic High School yearbook, 1972

Scott Redd, a 1972 class-mate who, along with his then-wife, befriended Sandra in the months before her death.

Olympic High School yearbook, 1972

Mark Perry in 1972—he was friendly with everyone at Olympic High.

Olympic High School yearbook, 1972

Sandra before her death in 2001.

Photo courtesy of John Joyner

Phillips Place apartments, where Sandra was living when she died. *Photo by Linda Seligman*

Sandra at a Carolina Panthers tailgate party with Gregg Pence shortly before her death. *Photo by Steve Pence*

Gregg Pence and James Niell at a tailgate party.
Photo courtesy of James Niell

Dr. Tucker's office at 300 Billingsley Road.

Sally after her arrest in 2006.

Courtesy of the Mecklenburg County Sheriff's Department

Calvary Church, where Sandra's family and friends gathered for her memorial service.

patient was in the recovery room and had been turned over to the recovery room nurse.

While Dr. Tucker was owner and principal of the Center for Cosmetic and Plastic Surgery clinic, his staff was acting as his agents/employees. As such, he was liable for all negligent acts and omissions that occur, according to the medical board.

But according to the nursing board's rules, nurse anesthetist are also charged with the responsibility for their patients. "The individual nurse anesthetist maintains accountability for the outcome of his or her actions," it states as part of 21-36.0226 Nurse Anesthesia Practice.

The September 2004 letter stated that Sally had been described by all the staff as an excellent CRNA, and they had indicated that they "would have been willing to allow her to put them to sleep, or one of their family members," prior to the April 10 incident.

Dr. Tucker fired Sally a month after Sandra's death. She had been a CRNA for twenty years; she had worked with Dr. Tucker at Presbyterian Hospital and moved with him to a three-doctor plastic surgery practice and then to his private practice nine years earlier.

During the malpractice hearing, it came out that Dr. Tucker and Sally had clearly disagreed on a number of office and surgery procedures.

Sally claimed that Dr. Tucker knew she had been administering pain medication, saying that she had been doing so for the nine years she had worked for him. But he was adamant that he did not know she was giving pain medications in the recovery room without authorization.

In sworn testimony, Dr. Tucker claimed that Sally was "incompetent"; however, there had not been any formal complaints about her job performance in the years they had worked together. The only indication of any problem was a note found in Dr. Tucker's office during the investigation that indicated that a couple of weeks prior to Sandra's death, a supervisor had talked to Sally about spending too much time in the recovery room and giving medications to patients while she was there. The note mentioned the fact that Sally had been giving medications in the recovery room without documenting them on the patient's record. It was not disclosed who had written the note, or if Dr. Tucker had seen it before Sandra's death.

During the investigation Sally said that the other nurses often asked her to administer pain medication, one nurse in particular. However, the nurse Sally said often asked her to give pain medications denied it when asked directly by the investigator. Sally said she had told Dr. Tucker early on that she was giving patients medications. And she was emphatic that the first time she'd administered fentanyl, she had told the doctor after the fact.

"I thought it was all right because the nurse said it was OK," Sally told the investigator.

After Sandra's death, Sally complained to friends that she felt like she was being set up, that it was being made to look like everything was her fault.

She didn't feel supported by Dr. Tucker when she claimed she was doing what he had said," a friend explained.

On Sally's medication audit sheet provided by the North Carolina Board of Nursing she indicated that she had administered fentanyl five times (for a total of 10 ccs) in the recovery room during the period from September 8, 2000, to May 10, 2001. The log included the 2 ccs she'd given Sandra Joyner in the recovery room. She had administered fentanyl forty-three times during surgery.

On several occasions the log indicated that Sally had written down one number and later changed it, but no reason for the change was documented.

On November 21, 2000, she documented signing out 4 ccs of fentanyl; 2 ccs were used in the operating room and 2 ccs were used in the post-anesthesia care unit, the log indicated. However, there is a note on the log saying that she'd originally signed out 2 ccs, then marked that out and documented 4 ccs.

Again on January 17, 2001, she signed out 4 ccs of fentanyl, and the log showed that 4 ccs were used, but there was a note saying she had only signed out 2 ccs. She had marked out 2 ccs and put "4 ccs."

It appeared that out of forty-three entries in the September 8, 2000–May 10, 2001, period, there were eleven changes to the log. It was also noted that on seven occasions a portion of the fentanyl, in increments of 1 ½ to 3 ccs, taken out of the lockbox, was listed as "wasted," but there was no witness to the disposal of it, as there should have been.

On May 9, 2001, there was a note saying a whole box of fentanyl had been dropped and 3 ccs had been wasted, again with no witness.

It was also puzzling that Sally had entered the wrong date on the anesthesia log, marking out "January 17, 2001" (the correct date), putting in "January 18."

The staff that was on duty the day Sandra died told the nursing board that Sally had been alone with the patient for only ten, maybe eleven minutes. They claimed they never actually saw her give the patient any medications, they merely saw her go in and out of the operating room to get supplies from her cart.

According to one of the surgical technicians, Sally was sitting at the counter eating during the time that Sandra was in trouble, when she was supposed to be watching her.

"One would not be alarmed that anything was wrong, because she was eating," the witness told the investigator.

Shortly after Sandra was settled in the recliner, the

surgical tech walked back into the operating room, but was still within sight and sound of the recovery room. She has said that she overheard Sandra say that her eyes were burning. Then Sandra began to draw up her knees in pain and asked Sally if she was being a bad patient.

The technician recalled Sally assuring Sandra that she was not being bad.

Sometime between 11:13 a.m. and 11:31 a.m., Sally said she administered 2 ccs of fentanyl, then Robinul and ephedrine, and Narcan, which is used to counteract an overdose of narcotic.

It was also noted that Sally had administered all of these IV medications in the recovery room without a consultation with Dr. Tucker.

One of the technicians mentioned to the investigator that Sally had also given the medications without documenting them on the patient's record.

A second technician told the investigator that when she glanced over at Sandra she noticed that her lips were bluish, but she knew Sandra had had a fat graft which could discolor the skin. "I glanced at the monitor and saw the number thirty-eight, but I don't know if it was the heart rate or what," she said. The tech then stepped closer and noted that Sandra's fingernails were blue. She asked Sally if the patient was OK. Then she pinched Sandra's toe to stimulate her.

"I walked over, patting her," she recalled.

The tech went on to say that the recovery room nurse came back into the room about that time and asked Sally if everything was OK.

"Fine," she had replied.

The co-worker reported that the recovery room nurse had lowered the head of the bed and placed an oxygen mask on Sandra. The patient had responded, so the recovery room nurse left the room again for a minute.

When she returned, it was apparent that the patient was not fine, said the nurse, so she went to get Dr. Tucker, who was in the room next door.

When asked what Sally was doing while all this was going on, the technician said, "I don't recall Sally doing anything but standing back. She seemed very calm. I did not at first realize that it was an emergency situation. Sally seemed fine. I asked if everything was OK and she said, 'Fine.'"

The recovery room nurse confirmed the same scenario. About 11:30 a.m., after getting the next patient, she had returned and noticed that Sandra's O_2 saturation was dropping, she told the investigator. "So I turned on the oxygen and gave it to Meredith [another tech] to put it on the patient. I immediately noticed her blood pressure was low."

When the tech asked Sally if she should get Dr. Tucker, Sally said, "No!"

But when she asked if she could put the patient's head down, Sally replied "All right."

The recovery room nurse told the investigator that it was when the patient's condition continued to deteriorate that she decided she needed to get Dr. Tucker.

As soon as Dr. Tucker arrived in the recovery room, emergency procedures were initiated.

Sally was just standing there, not doing anything, and not assisting in the resuscitative process, she added.

One of the surgical technicians remembered hearing Sally say repeatedly, "Take a deep breath," then she heard the recovery room nurse say the same thing. At that point another nurse came into the room and they all began working on Sandra.

A technician told the investigator that when she heard Dr. Tucker's voice in the room, she broke scrub and came out to help. When asked what Sally was doing during that period of time, that tech, too, reported that Sally was just standing there.

The staff told the investigator that the patient was then intubated and resuscitation methods were initiated, then EMS was called.

Throughout the process, all of the people who had been in the room told the investigator that Sally did not participate in the resuscitative process at all.

Although there had been a change in the patient's condition and Sandra had begun to deteriorate, Sally did not report the change to the physician as she was required to do, the technicians said.

When questioned by the investigator Sally told him that they had two surgeries scheduled the day of Sandra's death, one in the morning and one in the afternoon. Some days it would take six to eight hours for a single surgery if multiple procedures were involved, so they wouldn't schedule any other surgery; however, she told the investigator that on some days she was able to perform five breast augmentations, because they take less time to be completed than a facelift and other procedures which can total four or five hours each. Breast augmentations could be completed in about two hours.

When asked how she knew what the doctor's expectations were regarding her delivery of anesthesia, she said she had worked with him and three or four other physicians in an office setting. "I learned what was expected. Basically, the same as I would have done in a hospital."

When asked about the type of relationship she had with Dr. Tucker, she described it as "more collaborative," meaning that she was involved in the decision-making rather than just being a subordinate.

Sally said her responsibility was to get the patient to the recovery room, then get ready for the next patient.

"I always volunteered to stay with the patient, and the technician would go to prepare the next patient," she added.

She told the investigator that when the first patient of the day would come in for her appointment, the tech who was circulating and scrubbing would admit the patient, she would check the vital signs and give the patient a Valium. Sally would then go in and take the patient's history, discuss her general health and explain the anesthesia process to her.

"I would begin the IV and explain what I was doing, as well as give IV antibiotics. We would take the patient to the operating room and get vital signs. Then we would begin nasal oxygen and hook up the automatic blood pressure machine, the pulse oximeter and the EKG monitor," she said.

As soon as the doctor came in, Sally said she would begin the anesthesia. In the recovery room she would hook up the EKG monitor.

"I always got the first set of vital signs. I wrote it on my records and in theirs. Most of the time I could leave and go to the bathroom and get the next patient," she added.

Sally told the investigator that Sandra had arrived late and had been apprehensive.

Sally confirmed that she had known Sandra prior to the surgery, saying that the two had gone to junior high and high school together. She explained that they had merely been acquaintances.

Sally walked the investigator through the procedure once Sandra was in the recovery room, saying she was first helped into the big lounge chair and then a tech put ice packs on her eyes. But Sandra kept trying to get out of the chair, she added.

Sally said she told the tech, "I'm going to give her some fentanyl," which at first seemed to calm Sandra down.

When the investigator asked if it was common practice to give fentanyl in the recovery room, Sally replied, "It was normal practice to do that in 1998 [it is thought she meant 1999 when Sandra first had surgery]. My protocol was, when the nurses asked me, I did. I gave one cc, I only did it randomly."

Sally then told the investigator that the nurses had told her, "Dot [another nurse at the practice] does it all the time."

Later Sally told the investigator, "I have given fentanyl to hundreds of patients whose heart rates drop down and come back up." It is not clear whether she'd meant to say she gave Robinul and ephedrine to remedy heart rates, which is what they do, or if she'd actually meant fentanyl, which is a high-powered pain medication.

Sally reiterated that the first time she had given medication in the recovery room, she had told Dr. Tucker afterwards, and when asked how she determined that it would be OK to continue to give it, she stated, "He knew."

Sally insisted that the blood pressure monitor and pulse oximeter had been turned on during the time Sandra was complaining of face pain.

"What I remember is that the pulse oximeter fell off. I'd go and put it on. Amy [a staff nurse] was in and out, mostly out."

Sally acknowledged that she had been in the room alone with Sandra for only ten or eleven minutes. She said the surgical technician was in the operating room fixing her instruments.

"I gave one cc of fentanyl and then about five minutes later I gave a second one, another one cc. The problem started within a short period after the second one cc," she claimed.

"I noticed the pulse ox was off. The first thing I noticed was the pulse ox had dropped. I went and got Robinul and ephedrine. I keep it drawn up," Sally told the investigator.

Unfortunately, the use of Robinul, ephedrine and Narcan were not documented on the patient's record—which would have been especially important for the Narcan, which would have counteracted the pain medication overdose.

"The whole thing was like slow motion. One registered nurse happened to be in there and Linda [another RN] came in. We were all working together. The blood pressure came back up. They asked me if I needed Dr. Tucker," Sally told the investigator.

When Sally was asked what finally prompted someone to get the doctor when they weren't able to revive Sandra, she told the investigator a different story. "I asked the nurse to get him. Helen asked if she should call 911 and I said 'Yes.'"

That, of course, was not the same version her coworkers remembered. They said a nurse had gone to get Dr. Tucker in spite of Sally's statements that everything was OK, because it was apparent that the patient was not all right.

Later, when asked if it was possible that there had been a period of time when the patient was in trouble and she didn't realize it because she was eating, Sally stated emphatically, "No . . . after giving anesthesia for so long, I developed a sixth sense."

When questioned about when she would check vitals, Sally said she would check them every fifteen minutes in the recovery room. Later she told the investigator, "I watch [sic] them, but didn't actually go over and write them down."

When the investigator asked if Sally might have misjudged the seriousness of the situation because she was eating, Sally said, "I only got one bite [of her biscuit]" implying that she was not distracted by getting just that small amount of food.

At the end of the hearing, when the investigator asked if any discrepancies that had been found in documentation should be addressed, Sally said, "Oh, yes. If there were any, it was due to stupidity."

In her 2003 deposition, Sally admitted to the medical board that she'd known Sandra in junior high and high school.

"She was one of the judges of my cheerleading experience when I was in the eighth grade," she testified.

When the investigator asked whether she and Sandra had been friends, Hill said no and that she "would see her and her then-boyfriend [John] . . . walk around school together because he was in football and she was a cheerleader or letter girl, something like that."

Although neither Dr. Tucker nor Sally outwardly complained about their relationship, it became clear during the investigation that communication between them was not what it should have been. It wasn't clear whether everyone had the same difficulty with the doctor, or whether it was just Sally.

When asked if Sally thought she had done anything wrong that day, she said, "Not having better communication with Dr. Tucker. He would say 'You know how to give anesthesia, go do it.' When I went to tell him about problems, he just was like, 'Yeah, yeah, yeah.' He didn't want to hear it," Sally told the nursing board investigator.

Sally had admitted to friends that she was having a hard time with Dr. Tucker.

"I know he said during the deposition that he was not aware I was giving those drugs," Sally said. "That's totally not true," she said emphatically.

When the investigator asked Sally when she had first become aware that Sandra was in trouble, she said, "I noticed that the oxygen level had dropped, her lips and fingers were blue," adding that that was when she'd gone to her cart to get the Robinul and ephedrine, which she kept pre-mixed, just in case there was a problem.

When asked if she knew that everyone in the office had reported that she did nothing when the patient was clearly in trouble, that they said she kept on eating, even sitting on the counter at one point, Sally's answer was even more confusing.

"No, I even had a friend who has a friend who works there, and it was said I was sitting there drinking coffee and eating while she [the patient] was arresting. All I know was, only Sandra Joyner, me and Jesus were there, and we know what happened."

When asked why she didn't check vital signs and write them down like she was supposed to do, Sally's response sounded even more cavalier.

"I watched them, but didn't actually go over and write them down. When you've been doing this as long as I have, you know when someone is in trouble. I know [sic] that the patient was in trouble."

Hill was clearly distraught when Sandra couldn't be resuscitated by Dr. Tucker and EMTs. In fact, she told the office manager, "It was all my fault."

Sally admitted to the investigator that she was upset about Sandra's death; friends said she'd been grief-stricken over it. "She was crushed and devastated for a year," said a friend who'd gone through those trying times with Sally.

But even as Sally related the April 10 events to the investigator, her concerns seem to be somehow focused on herself rather than her patient.

"I didn't go to the hospital. I wanted to, but he [Dr.

Tucker] didn't want me to. It makes me mad now, because I wish I had gone. . . ."

When asked if she could have done anything differently that day, her reply was startling: "I can't think of anything I'd do different. Honest to God, I'd not do anything different," she repeated.

After the investigation, the nursing board spelled out Sally's nursing act violations and made recommendations as to how the matter could be resolved. The board determined that Sally had seven violations:

— She had engaged in conduct that endangered public health;
— She was unfit or incompetent to practice nursing by reason of deliberate or negligent acts or omissions in which actual injury to the patient was established;
— She had engaged in conduct that deceived, defrauded, or harmed the public in the course of professional activities or services;
— She had violated a provision of this Article;
— She had willfully violated rules enacted by the Board;
— She was at fault for not making available to another healthcare professional's client information that was crucial to the safety of Sandra's health care;
— She had failed to maintain an accurate record for her client that contained all pertinent healthcare information.

In the report the board outlined options that Sally had for resolution of the infractions.

She was entitled to an administrative hearing before a majority of the members of the board of nursing or its designated hearing officer. At that time she would be given the opportunity to present sworn testimony, arguments and evidence regarding the allegations against her. If she wanted to pursue that avenue, the report said, a hearing would be scheduled within a reasonable time period.

She or her attorney would be required to sign every document that had been filed with the board of nursing.

As a result of their findings, the board also proposed several sanctions against Sally Hill.

She would have to voluntarily surrender her license for one year and prior to consideration for reinstatement of it, she would have to successfully complete a board-approved ethical/legal decision-making course.

At the time of a request for reinstatement of her license, she would have to appear before the licensure committee and present evidence that she was safe and competent to practice nursing.

During the time of her suspension Sally could not be listed as a Nurse Aide II and the board of nursing would recommend to the Division of Facility Services that she not be listed as a Nurse Aide I.

The nursing board informed her that their action would be public information, saying that the board posts a list of persons who have received disciplinary action on the North Carolina Board of Nursing website.

A consent form to accept the proposed discipline was included with the letter, asking that her wallet-sized nursing license be attached to the form and mailed back to them. A complete list of courses she might attend would be sent once the board received her completed consent form. Sally had ten days to respond.

In September 2004, as requested, Sally voluntarily submitted her nursing license, but she never requested that it be reinstated. In fact, she told family and friends that as she was still suffering from the effects of her chemotherapy, she didn't think she would ever be able to return to nursing.

Said one friend, "After her second chemotherapy she was living with the backlash of the chemicals and memory loss. She was on disability. She never tried to get her license back because she didn't feel like she would ever be able to go back to nursing."

FIFTEEN

Perspectives

According to Chris Bettin, a spokesperson for the American Association of Nurse Anesthetists in Florida, there has never been another case like the one involving Sally Hill.

He confirms that the people who choose to become certified nurse anesthetists are detail-oriented; they want to be in control and generally are, as far as their area of expertise.

The practice of nurse anesthesia has been around for a long time. Nurse anesthetists were the first professionals in the country to provide anesthesia, long before doctors were trained in the specialty. It has also been one of the most aggressive fields to improve favorable outcomes, he added.

Statistics indicate that in the 1980s there were two anesthesia-related deaths for every 250,000 surgeries; in 1999 those statistics had dropped to one in every 250,000.

The association has reported that there are currently 36,000 nurse anesthetists in the country. And the nursing board, which says there are 120,000 nurses (including nurse anesthetists), takes action on about 280 complaints a year.

According to the North Carolina Board of Nursing, a

nurse anesthetist is required to be supervised by a primary physician, but that practice is constantly being reviewed and revised. To date fourteen states have opted out of the rule of having a physician supervise the nurse anesthetist, and North Carolina is one of thirty-one states considering the opt out. To "opt out" of the requirement, the governor must consult with the state board of nursing and medicine to determine if removing supervision is consistent with state law and in the best interests of the citizens. Once these requirements are met, the governor can write a letter to the Centers for Medicare & Medicaid Services requesting the "opt out." However, it is a lengthy process and many states, including North Carolina, have maintained the status quo.

As the industry has changed and more plastic surgery is being done in clinics with a certified nurse anesthetist, a debate has surfaced over the use of nurse anesthetists instead of medical anesthetists. The difference is that a registered nurse can earn an anesthesiology certification while a medical anesthetist has a medical degree with additional training in anesthesiology. At the heart of the debate is the fact that a medical anesthetist has a six-year medical degree before studying anesthesia; an RN can become a certified nurse anesthetist in three to four years. The issue has been hotly debated in North Carolina.

"Whenever new slots open in the medical profession, physicians feel like the new disciplines are trying to practice medicine without a license," said an industry spokesperson. "Basically, it cuts into their territory."

While anesthesia often gets the blame for complications, death can, of course, sometimes be caused by surgeon error or an allergic reaction to medication.

Bettin encourages the public to question everyone involved in their surgery.

"Personally meet everyone who will be working on

you, ask questions about their experience—if they are board-certified, what type of emergency procedures are in place, what they have on their crash cart."

Cindy Martin of Durham, North Carolina, who has been a certified nurse anesthetist for ten years, has worked with Duke University Medical Center and Durham Regional Hospital and is currently an independent contractor for four plastic surgeons. She found it difficult to comprehend how so many things could have gone wrong the day Sandra died. She is, in fact, convinced that Sandra's life could easily have been saved.

Cindy, who graduated from the Raleigh School of Nurse Anesthesia and received a master's degree from the University of North Carolina at Greensboro where she graduated cum laude, has also been an instructor. She, like many others, has questioned the use of fentanyl as a pain medication after surgery.

"I wouldn't give a patient two ccs of fentanyl in the recovery room at Duke University Medical Center, where there are a zillion people around to watch them. It's a hundred times more potent than morphine," she explained.

Typically fentanyl is used in the IV sedation before surgery begins, with only ½ cc dispensed at a time until it is apparent that the patient is under, she said. Nurse anesthetists are always extremely cautious when using it. "The number one consideration in giving fentanyl is that a patient might have respiratory arrest with it," she explained. "It is the first precaution listed in the *Physicians' Desk Reference*."

One reason it is a drug of choice in the operating room is that it is so powerful, but that is also the reason it is not generally used as pain medication after surgery unless the patient has a chronic disease or is someone with a high tolerance for pain medication. "In that case, giving them morphine would be like giving them water," she added.

Cindy also says it is customary to chart the vitals of someone in the recovery room every five minutes in the beginning, not every fifteen minutes. It is critical that the nurse anesthetist write the vitals down on the patient's record. " 'If you didn't write it down, you didn't do it,' we always say. And our mantra is 'Monitor, monitor, monitor.' We take our jobs very seriously . . . we are managing a person's life."

In examining Sandra's case, Cindy was puzzled by the many changes on the medication log. In her experience a nurse anesthetist might occasionally need to change the log that tracks the narcotics that she used, maybe two changes out of twenty-five.

Out of forty-three items on Sally's log (February through May 2001), almost every entry had been changed: ten times she'd changed the amount of fentanyl that was used; seven times she'd indicated that fentanyl had been wasted, but there was no witness. On one occasion she'd entered the wrong date for the day she had taken the fentanyl, on another she'd shown no total for how much anesthesia had been used that day. And on May 9, 2001, she'd indicated that a box of fentanyl had been dropped and 3 ccs wasted, again with no witness.

According to her log sheet, out of forty-three surgeries, Sally had administered fentanyl five times in the recovery room.

Most unbelievable, Cindy says, is the fact that a nurse anesthetist would be remiss in making sure a pulse oximeter was not on a patient's finger with the alarm turned on at all times."

"Why would you put one on a patient without an alarm?" she asked rhetorically. "The pulse oximeter is critical, it can dig you out of a big hole. If there is a reaction to the narcotics, it will sound the alarm immediately if something goes wrong."

The device, she said, measures the oxygen saturation of a patient's blood; if oxygen is getting to the finger, it is getting to the brain. Because of the pulse oximeter's simplicity and speed, the ones that clip onto a patient's finger are generally used. They also display the results within a few seconds. Generally acceptable normal ranges for oxygen saturation are from 95 to 100 percent.

Pulse oximeters are a critical part of emergency medicine and are also useful for patients with respiratory or cardiac problems. It is vital to know how much oxygen is getting to a patient's brain at all times. If a patient is having trouble breathing, it must immediately be done artificially or by a mechanical ventilation, otherwise brain damage and cardiac arrest can occur.

"The number two fear for nurse anesthetists is that the pulse oximeter will fail to work, because it can literally save someone's life. If there had been an alarm on the pulse oximeter, Sally would have heard it beeping and she would have been able to save the woman's life," says Cindy. Detective Henson has said that Sally admitted turning off the alarm. During the hearing board investigation she said the pulse ox fell off.

Cindy also stresses the importance of administering fentanyl ½ cc at a time, and says that even with that low dose, the patient can still go apneic. If the patient is inadvertently given too much medication and goes into respiratory arrest, it is imperative that the nurse anesthetist administer Narcan immediately and run a full code.

"Sally should have been supporting Sandra's airways when she went into respiratory arrest. She was trying to take care of numbers, but she wasn't fixing the reason for the problems. She needed to get Sandra's oxygen up even if she had to use an ambu bag. If she had been breathing for her, Sandra wouldn't have coded."

John O'Donnell, who heads up the nurse anesthetist

program at the University of Pittsburgh, agrees. "Seventy-five percent of fentanyl is taken up by the lungs. It's what gets to the brain that causes the adverse effect."

One of his students encountered the same situation as Sally when he inadvertently gave a patient too much pain medication during his first surgery.

"I realized it immediately. The student determined that the patient should be ventilated immediately and a new tube put in. As a result there was no negative outcome," O'Donnell added.

Clearly there should always be rapid intervention with any problem, he added. "If the patient is having any type of trouble—oxygen levels drop, blood pressure is erratic, or the patient has tachycardia—it should be countered immediately."

In the case of Sandra Joyner, she was given Robinul and ephedrine when it became clear she was in distress, but it is not known when or if Sandra was given Narcan initially.

"If the patient is having respiratory problems due to an overdose of pain medication, the nurse anesthetist knows to immediately administer Narcan, one or two milligrams at a time. If the patient has stopped breathing, they should be given the entire vial at one time," he added.

Cindy Martin agreed. "You can tell when someone is overnarcotized. If you don't offset the overdose immediately, they go into respiratory arrest and they likely have cardiac arrest and die."

It is odd, said Cindy, that the patient had been left alone in the recovery room, regardless of how brief a time it was. "We never leave a patient alone under any circumstances, and the patient should always be wearing a pulse oximeter the entire time. If you need to step out of the recovery room, you have someone else watch the patient."

She even tells families not to leave a patient alone for

twenty-four hours after their surgery when they have returned home; in fact the family has to sign a piece of paper to that effect, saying they won't even go to the store.

Caregivers will be taking narcotics home to give to the recuperating patient. Cindy stresses the importance of not giving the patient a medication and walking away; she said they need to make sure the patient gets up and goes to the bathroom over the next twenty-four hours and reminds them that someone is on call around the clock if they should have questions or concerns.

An example of why it's so important for caregivers to follow these instructions is the recent death of Donda West, Kanye West's mother, who, it appears from news reports, may have died from too much pain medication after going home from having a breast reduction and tummy tuck. By the time she was taken to the hospital, she couldn't be revived.

Bottom line, Cindy believes that on April 10, because of all the fatal errors, "That woman just seemed destined to die that day."

Others firmly believe Sandra Joyner died because of Sally's incompetence.

"She just didn't do enough," said Mark Perry, a high school friend who has worked as a private investigator.

Dr. Barry Freidberg, an expert anesthesiologist who has promoted the safe use of anesthetics in over thirty articles and has written a book for doctors on the subject says, "Fentanyl should only be given on a short-term basis. If a patient has been given five ccs during surgery, she is in danger if given two ccs more in the recovery room, because now it has been used for the long-term."

In fact, he said, "She's lucky she wasn't dead after the five ccs. Giving her two more was like putting a gun to her head."

Cindy prefers to err on the side of being too conservative when giving any narcotic. "My philosophy is that you can give more, but you can't take it back. That's why I only give it one-half cc at a time. If the patient is still in pain, I give another one-half cc. If you give them more and can't undo it, there is a risk of respiratory arrest, which I've never had, and ultimately they go into cardiac arrest. Fortunately, all of my patients have been breathing and happy in recovery. Not one has had difficulty because of medication or respiratory arrest."

On the whole, nurse anesthetists are fully aware of the burden that rests on their shoulders. "Whatever goes wrong in surgery, it is generally the anesthetic that gets the blame."

Although nurse anesthesists' jobs are stressful, there are also some healthy rewards for their responsibility. Nurse anesthetists' salaries are generally around $160,000 in a hospital or clinic. Independent contractors like Sally can make upwards of $250,000.

It is Cindy's theory that had any one of several procedures—careful administering of a narcotic, proper monitoring by a pulse oximeter with an alarm or quick response if respiratory failure was indicated—been used, Sandra's life could have been saved.

Without a doubt, had Narcan been administered in a timely manner or the doctor been called immediately when it became evident Sandra was in trouble, the outcome would have been different. To have so many things go wrong seems incongruous with the nature of a nurse anesthetist, she explains.

"The professional norm is that they are detail-oriented and naturally sticklers for patient safety," explains John O'Donnell.

Cindy's assessment is a little stronger. "There's no doubt we [nurse anesthetists] are control freaks. Sometimes nurse anesthetists try to convey the attitude of 'I've got it under control' when they don't. In this case, I would say this lady died for no reason."

Dr. Friedberg shared those feelings, saying he finds that anesthetists have an "attitude thing." "Anesthetists will oftentimes lead the patient to think they are a physician," he said.

Cindy said emphatically that in case of an emergency it is the nurse anesthetist who should be in charge. "We are the ones to get the ambu [rescue] bag, we are the 'queens of the airways.'"

The nurse anesthetist would also be the one to "run the code," because if the patient goes into respiratory arrest, it is likely they will also have cardiac arrest.

For four to five years, a nurse anesthetist receives extensive training about what to do in case of an emergency, hoping she will never have one.

"We set the tone in the room. I might be freaked out, but while I appear calm, I'll be barking orders. We've certainly been taught how to work under pressure." Instead, Cindy said it appears as though several procedures failed that fateful day in 2001: the missing pulse oximeter alarm, Sally's slow action to attend to the respiratory arrest and the lack of emergency procedures all provided "the perfect storm."

"She may have been accustomed to doing things in a sloppy manner," Cindy said thoughtfully.

"But any way you look at it, it all comes down to incompetence," concluded Martin about Sally's actions that day.

SIXTEEN

Tucker's Suspicions

In sworn testimony that Dr. Tucker made before the North Carolina Medical Board, which wasn't made public until three years later when a ruling was changed that allowed the deposition to be released to *The Charlotte Observer*, it became apparent that from the very beginning, he'd thought Sally's actions on April 10, 2001, went far beyond negligence.

Fortunately, Karen Garloch at the *Observer* published most of the salient points of the deposition. A North Carolina law that has since been passed now prohibits release of the deposition to anyone else.

According to the *Observer*, during the 2003 hearing, Dr. Tucker told the medical board that Sally had been a "rogue nurse," who had acted without his instructions. "I think there is an element of malicious behavior here," he said emphatically.

In a stunning disclosure, Dr. Tucker was also reported to have said that after finally being summoned by another nurse, Sally met him at the door of the recovery room. When he asked her what was wrong, he was startled by her response.

"She looked at me . . . and she stomped her foot," he told the panel.

Dr. Tucker said he realized Sally was "not in control of what was going on," so he "swept her out of the way" and tried to resuscitate the patient himself.

"The Sally Hill that I knew was not there when I walked into the room," he testified. "I don't know if she had a mental lapse. I don't know if she snapped."

In Dr. Tucker's 135-page deposition, he made several points that now seem to be the basis for the murder charges Sally is facing.

In it, the *Observer* reported that Dr. Tucker alleged that Sally had attached Sandra to an electrocardiogram (EKG) machine, which he says might have led the staff to wrongly believe her breathing was normal because it makes a beeping sound that is similar to the pulse oximeter. John O'Donnell says the patient is often hooked up to the pulse oximeter and EKG machine in the recovery room. And it is difficult to understand how the two measurements could be confused, because the pulse oximeter is a clamp that is placed on the forefinger and an EKG is attached to a patient's chest with pads or alligator clips. But again, they both make a beeping sound.

Dr. Tucker also said that Sally had administered a high dose of fentanyl to the recovering patient without his permission.

In spite of the fact that Dr. Tucker made it clear all along that he believed Sally had committed a "criminal act," neither the medical nor nursing boards that investigated Sandra's death had accused Sally of any intentional wrongdoing.

"I think that's a rogue nurse on her own wild mustang riding through the West, you know, shooting whoever she wants," Dr. Tucker reportedly told the medical board. "This is way out of what we would ever expect or think anybody would do."

Dr. Tucker has privately said that he reported his

suspicions to the district attorney's office. The only explanation that has been given is that nothing was done because the medical examiner had ruled Sandra's death an accident.

SEVENTEEN

A Deadly Mix

The mention of high potency drugs has become so commonplace that the general public often assumes they are safe, especially when administered or prescribed by a physician. The many settings in which they can be abused is an even bigger story that often doesn't make the headlines.

The use of drugs for medical and non-medical purposes has been traced back to man's early history by Aldous Huxley, who said, "Pharmacology is older than agriculture."

It is interesting to note that until the 19th century, drugs came from two sources—unrefined plants and animal products. And they were usually taken by only one route of administration—oral ingestion, eating a crude plant material, or compounds.

Around 1000 A.D., distillation techniques were applied to fermented beverages. In the mid-1800s morphine was isolated from opium; in the early 1900s cocaine was derived from the coca leaf and heroin was synthesized from morphine. The abuse of these purified, more potent materials soon followed.

A highly potent synthetic narcotic, fentanyl (or phentanyl) was first created in 1960 by Dr. Paul Janssen for a

Belgian company called Janssen Pharmaceutica. Although the compound was discovered in 1960, it was not released to the public until 1963.

Fentanyl is generally used to relieve moderate to severe pain, and to control pain during labor, and following surgery and other procedures. The drug is also used to induce and maintain anesthesia and sedation during surgery.

But fentanyl is not only used in the medical world; it is an illegal street drug. It is an opiate, and the effects are almost exactly the same as those of heroin. While Europe had fentanyl in the 1960s, it did not reach the U.S. until 1970. Shortly thereafter its illegal use began.

Not long after, another form of fentanyl was discovered, the one that is widely used today, fentanyl citrate, which allows patients to have very fast pain relief.

Today fentanyl is used in patches, a delivery system that has been lauded as an innovative way to deliver relief of chronic pain without relying on injections or complicated pills. The patch is attached directly to the skin, where it releases a constant amount of the drug for seventy-two hours, according to health officials.

However, there have been some bad batches. In 2004 a number of shipments of the patches had to be recalled because they caused several accidental deaths in Los Angeles County alone. There was a warning about the patches in 2005, two alerts in 2007 and two recalls in 2008.

In fact the *Los Angeles Times* has reported claims of as many as 230 deaths because of the patches in the last six years, and the FDA is investigating 130 more.

There are also fentanyl lollipops for children, a raspberry lozenge attached to a handle that must be swabbed inside the mouth and gums to be absorbed.

Prior to human consumption, fentanyl (called carfentanil) was used in veterinary medicine to immobilize large animals. In 1979 a scandal erupted when fentanyl was given to racehorses so that they would not be slowed down by their injuries and pain. As a result, owners and trainers were fined and/or suspended.

In 2002 fentanyl was used by a Russian security force to incapacitate rebels in the Moscow theater siege.

When used illegally, fentanyl is most often injected, but it can also be smoked or snorted. Several years ago it was sold on the street as "China White" or "Starsky and Hutch." Today Actiq is being sold on the streets and is called "percopop."

According to the New York Bureau of Narcotic Enforcement website, "Fentanyl is most often diverted by those healthcare professionals directly responsible for its administration and safeguarding . . . primarily from operating rooms."

The bureau says this is done by substitution, outright theft, the underdosing of surgical patients, and the falsifying of medication administration records. Fentanyl patches are often stolen from ward stocks or actually removed from the skin of the patients. The patch is then punctured or sliced open to extract the fentanyl.

Whatever the method of the diversion, if abused, fentanyl can be a danger to the public health. And impaired healthcare professionals pose enormous potential consequences for patients. In fact, says the bureau, a patient's life can be placed in jeopardy.

Fentanyl is a narcotic analgesic. It relieves pain without the patient losing consciousness, much like morphine and oxycontin.

Basically it makes the user feel intensely happy. However the feeling is often followed by some of the negative side effects: dizziness, light-headedness, shortness of breath, anxiety and hearing/feeling things that are not there.

In the case of an overdose, the person has cold

clammy skin, severe dizziness and drowsiness, and trouble breathing.

Fentanyl is preferred in an IV for surgery because of its very prompt onset of action and short duration. But like other narcotic analgesics, respiratory depression is the most significant acute toxic effect. The depth and duration of respiratory depression depends on the analog used and the dose administered. As with other narcotics, naloxone (Narcan) is the antidote of choice if respiratory depression does occur.

While considered a boon to pain relief during surgery, the fact that it is one of the most potent drugs ever created makes it one of the most abused drugs in the country.

In 2003, a Bradenton, Florida, mother of three was found dead in the bathroom of her home from an overdose of alcohol, fentanyl and cocaine.

"Anybody can get it [fentanyl] with a prescription," said Dr. Daniel Spitz, the Bradenton medical examiner.

Drugs dispensed through pharmacies can be another danger. At least a dozen states have enacted new laws or regulations in the past year that require pharmacists to report medication errors. Five more states have tried and failed, but will likely try again.

At this point North Carolina is the only state that requires serious medication errors to be reported to a pharmacy board. Executive director of the North Carolina Board of Pharmacy David Work said the board has been investigating all North Carolina deaths involving drugs dispensed through pharmacies for about a decade. It received about forty-five Rx–drug-related fatality reports in 2002, he said.

"These reports don't take a lot of time for pharmacists," he said. "We look at what happened and why, not who might be involved. No-fault reporting is absolutely vital."

Connecticut requires prescribers, pharmacists and pharmacy technicians to report even a reasonable suspicion of a medication error, but not to the pharmacy board. Error reports go to the state's Commissioner of Consumer Protection, who must consult with the board pharmacy. Consumer protection officials can then launch an investigation independently of the board.

California is taking a different approach. All pharmacies must have a formal method to track, reduce and report medication errors. Errors must be reported to the provider and the patient, not the board of pharmacy. Every error must be investigated within forty-eight hours of discovery and every investigation must result in a formal report. The report must be maintained in the pharmacy for at least a year.

Nevada is casting a wider net. A tort reform and medication error bill signed into law in August 2002 requires anyone employed by a medical facility to report any questionable event, including significant medication errors. Reports go to the patient safety officer at the facility who reports the event to the state health division.

When a patient is planning to have surgery, they generally check out the credentials of the surgeon, but never give a moment's thought to the safety practices employed by the clinic and its staff.

After Sandra Joyner's death, Dr. Tucker's office was cited for sloppy office procedures, lack of emergency procedures and inadequate patient files, all internal operations that a patient would have no way of checking on.

If the office had been run the way it should have been, could Sandra's death have been prevented?

EIGHTEEN

Fentanyl Problems

This is certainly not the first time fentanyl has caused a death and made the headlines.

In 2001, 26-year-old Greg deVillers was found dead on the floor in his California home. A photo of his wedding, taken less than two years earlier, and a crumpled love letter lay nearby—a letter to his wife, Kristin Rossum, from the dashing Australian doctor who was her boss at the San Diego Medical Examiner's Office. Beside the letter was Kristin's journal, in which she'd written that she feared that her marriage had been a mistake.

On the surface, it seemed an obvious suicide. Broken-hearted over his wife's affair, unwilling to face the future without her, deVillers had taken his own life.

But in what would become known as the Rose Petal Murder Mystery, authorities would come to suspect that deVillers' own wife, a 26-year-old blonde beauty, the daughter of well-respected university professors, used the knowledge she had gained as a toxicologist for the medical examiner's office to poison her unsuspecting husband with a deadly cocktail of drugs.

Among the narcotics found in his system was fentanyl. It was a drug, authorities would later say, that Rossum knew her own office never tested for and which she believed medical examiners would never detect.

"It was the perfect poison," Deputy San Diego District Attorney David Hendron has said.

Investigators had to follow a twisted trail of drugs, lies and sex for eight months. The presence of that much fentanyl alone wasn't enough to make a murder case, Hendron had said. It was still possible that Rossum was right when she suggested that deVillers had taken his own life by overdosing on the drug.

But if deVillers had intentionally taken that much fentanyl, he would have fallen unconscious almost instantly. He never would have had time to dispose of the container the drug had been in. It was also determined that his lungs had filled with fluid, meaning he had been unconscious for a minimum of six to twelve hours before he finally died.

Then word of Rossum's earlier drug abuse leaked out. Investigators found that a small amount of methamphetamine was missing from the office's drug locker. Fifteen fentanyl patches and one vial of the drug in its powdered form were also gone from the locker, to which Rossum had the key.

That discovery became more intriguing when authorities learned that all sixteen samples were from cases Rossum had worked on.

But what probably cinched charges against her were inconsistencies in her story. She said she found her husband lying dead on the floor with the rose petals, letters, photo and journal found near him.

In contradictory testimony, paramedics said that was strange, because when they'd rolled the unresponsive man over, they'd found no rose petals beneath him.

They later learned she had used a credit card to purchase a single rose that same day. Though she would later insist it had been for her lover, authorities felt sure the petals scattered over deVillers' body had come from that single red rose.

On November 13, 2002, more than two years after deVillers' death, a three-week murder trial ended with Rossum being convicted of first-degree murder with special circumstances. On December 12, she was sentenced to life in prison without parole.

At Downstate Medical Center in Brooklyn, Jennifer Timbrook was found dead in a radiology darkroom at Kings County Hospital. Her body was sprawled a few feet from two syringes believed to have contained fentanyl.

Jennifer Timbrook, 32, a student, was discovered when a hospital employee noticed the darkroom door was locked. Authorities have indicated that there was no "evidence of foul play." They believe Timbrook died from an overdose of fentanyl. They were trying to determine where the drug had come from and if it had been taken from the hospital's supply.

It was not clear whether the overdose was accidental or intentional, though no suicide note was found.

Beryl Williams, a hospital spokeswoman said the hospital adheres to stringent guidelines to prevent the theft of dangerous medications.

"There are certain kinds of drugs kept under lock and key, and only doctors and nurses can sign for them," Williams said. "If a drug isn't all used up, it has to be discarded. Our students do not have access to those kinds of drugs."

Police investigators said they were looking into whether the drugs had been taken from a Kings County storage area or disposal container.

But even when drugs, including fentanyl, are kept under lock and key, statistics show that they can be used and abused by medical staff, and often go unnoticed until the person is out of control.

As stringent as the guidelines are, they can't always prevent theft, especially if a staff member is addicted to the narcotic.

NINETEEN

Plastic Surgery on the Rise

In the last few years plastic surgery has become increasingly affordable and more popular for everyday people, not just the wealthy and celebrities.

Los Angeles has long been the number one location where plastic surgery procedures take place, but just recently a local TV station discovered that Charlotte, North Carolina, is number two, leading them to title a piece "Charlotte's Dirty Little Secret."

In 2005 11.5 million cosmetic surgeries and non-surgical procedures were performed in the U.S., which accounted for $9.4 billion, and the numbers increase every year, according to the American Society for Aesthetic Plastic Surgery.

Today cosmetic surgery is a $9.4 billion business.

Among the most popular procedures are liposuction (using suction to remove fat from specific areas of the body such as the stomach or thighs), with 455,489 performed in 2005; breast augmentation (enhancement of the breasts using either saline or silicone gel prosthetics), 364,610 in 2005; blepharoplasty (reshaping the eyelids), 231,467; rhinoplasty (reshaping the nose), 200,924; and breast reduction (reducing the size, generally because they are painful).

Other cosmetic surgeries like the "tummy tuck"(reshaping and firming of the abdomen); butt augmentation (using silicone implants to reshape); mastopexy (reshaping and lifting the breasts); and chin augmentation with silicone implants, are also becoming more commonplace.

In recent years, a growing number of patients have begun seeking cosmetic surgery in countries like Cuba, Thailand, Argentina, India and some areas of Europe, where the procedures can be done for up to 50 percent less than it costs in the U.S. But the risk of complications and the lack of after-surgery support is often overlooked by those simply looking for the cheapest option.

Not surprisingly, women make up approximately 87 percent of the population having cosmetic surgery, men approximately 11 percent. People in the 35–50 age range have the most procedures done, next to 19–24-year-olds at approximately 24 percent. People over age 65 or under 18, who are not the best candidates for plastic surgery, make up only approximately 3 percent of the plastic surgery population.

As more and more clinics use aggressive marketing tactics to attract clients, it has become even more important for consumers to do their homework and proceed cautiously. Before undergoing any cosmetic procedure, it is important for the patient to check references, find out about the doctor and the clinic, and the qualifications of its employees.

While we hear more about plastic cosmetic surgery now, and there is less shame in having it done, plastic surgery itself has actually been around quite a while.

The word "plastic" is derived from the Greek *plastikos*, meaning to mold or to shape. Plastic surgeons typically mold and reshape tissues of the body: bone, cartilage, muscle, fat and skin.

The history of plastic surgery dates back to 700 BC and

the physicians of ancient India, where skin grafts were utilized for reconstructive work.

The Romans performed simple operations, such as repairing damaged ears, around the 1st century BC. In the mid–15th century in Europe, Heinrich von Pfolspeundt told of a process "to make a new nose, removing skin from the arm and suturing it in place.

However it was not until the 19th and 20th centuries that plastic surgery became commonplace.

The U.S.'s first plastic surgeon, Dr. John Peter Mettauer performed the first cleft palate operation in 1827 with special instruments that he designed himself. New Zealand otolaryngologist Sir Harold Gillies developed many of the techniques of modern plastic surgery when treating facial injuries in World War I. One of his former students and a cousin expanded upon his work during World War II, pioneering treatments for RAF airmen suffering from severe burns.

Dr. Vilray Blair, one of the founders of the specialty, served as the first chief of the Division of Plastic and Reconstructive Surgery at Washington University in St. Louis. Blair treated complex maxillofacial injuries of World War I soldiers, and his paper "Reconstructive Surgery of the Face" was the landmark work for craniofacial reconstruction. He was also one of the first non-oral surgeons elected to the American Association of Oral and Plastic Surgery, later renamed the American Association of Plastic Surgeons.

Now cosmetic surgery is so commonplace that it has become a sought-after gift—breast enhancements for a girl's 18th birthday; facelifts for a woman's 25th wedding anniversary; liposuction for a man's new executive position. At one time only celebrities and the wealthy could afford to have plastic surgery, now it is more affordable, and people can even finance it.

In Sandra's case—for her mini-facelift, fat grafts and laser surgery—the tab ranged around $12,000–$14,000, which is not too much to pay to look like the person you used to be, and to regain your self-esteem.

The reason a person's looks become so important as we age is simple. In general, facial expressions and appearance convey what and how a person feels. But as the face ages, the skin loses its elasticity and firmness, and the face is prone to sagging and wrinkles.

Even though a person may be energetic and excited about life, the aging process can make them appear tired and unhappy, which affects the way they feel about themselves and how others see them.

Sagging in the middle of the face often creates a deep crease below the lower eyelid (called a tear trough) and between the nose and mouth (nasolabial fold) that may make someone in middle age appear tired and sad. Fat that has fallen or is displaced and loss of muscle tone in the lower face can also create jowls. The loss of youthful contours in the mid-face, jawline and neck areas are due to a variety of factors including heredity, gravity, environmental conditions and stress.

A facelift is designed to correct the sagging facial skin and muscles by removing excess fat and restoring firmness to create a more youthful, rested and vibrant appearance. The procedure is a restorative surgery—it does not change the fundamental appearance of a person's face and it cannot stop the aging process, according to information distributed by the American Association of Plastic Surgeons.

In some cases a mini-facelift can be done in place of a traditional standard facelift. A mini-facelift is safer because it is less invasive and does not require general anesthesia, although it is available if a patient requests it.

A mini-facelift has a much faster recovery period and

costs less, which makes it more available to a wide range of patients.

But there is risk involved with any kind of surgery, especially in regard to anesthesia, or if the patient has any kind of underlying health problem.

"Surgery is surgery. In an office or hospital there is always inherent risk, usually because of the anesthesia," said a retired Charlotte plastic surgeon.

There are four grades of anesthesia that can be used. Patients who usually seek plastic surgery are most often in Class I with no risk factors. Class II patients may have a health condition such as heart problems or high blood pressure, but medication has corrected it.

Patients with Class III and IV conditions are riskier, and surgery is not done in the office, but in a hospital. Sometimes doctors won't even agree to perform the procedure at all.

According to a local plastic surgeon, when death from plastic surgery does occur, it is generally due to pulmonary embolism, a clot that forms in the legs and breaks loose and goes to the lungs. "That's a problem with any kind of surgery, and generally happens after the patient has gone home," he explained.

The second cause of death from plastic surgery is when the patient develops an airway problem, which can easily happen with rhinoplasty, for instance, when blood goes down the throat and the patient chokes, or when anesthesia causes blood to get into the windpipe.

The number three cause of death is when drug reactions occur.

The same surgeon explained that there is rarely cardiac arrest or stroke, particularly with plastic surgery.

Back in the 1980s, when anesthesia was becoming more advanced for outpatient procedures, and more surgery was being performed in the office instead of the hospital, there

was a string of deaths in Florida, mostly the result of liposuction procedures.

It was during that time that the American Association for
Accreditation of Ambulatory Surgical Facilities (AAAASF)
was established to help make plastic surgery done in an office safer. Today it is estimated that over half of all cosmetic surgeries are performed in an office facility.

In the 1980s, no data on plastic surgery–related deaths
was being tracked, but now the AAAASF stays on top of
safety issues. It inspects, certifies and credits office-based
operating facilities to make sure every possible safety
procedure is followed around the country.

Anyone who is a member of AAAASF must be certified or else the facility will lose its membership. Since the
organization was formed, it has been collecting data on a
variety of situations such as deaths, complications, and
other occurrences.

The association, which reports a death rate of .05 percent, is thought to have the best possible figures—even
better than hospitals—because hospitals don't follow up
on plastic surgery patients once they leave.

Dr. Peter Tucker's Center for Cosmetic and Plastic Surgery has been a member of AAAASF since 2002; records
were not being kept in 2001 when Sandra Joyner died.

As outpatient surgery has increased, more certified
registered nurse anesthetists are being used to administer
sedation instead of medical anesthetists, who have a medical degree and generally work in hospitals. The issue has
become a bone of contention, especially in the state of
North Carolina.

"It is infinitely more efficient to do it [plastic surgery]
in the office. But who oversees it has been a contentious
issue," explained one plastic surgeon.

In 1986 legislation was passed by Congress that made
the field of certified nurse anesthetists the first nursing

specialty to be directly reimbursed under the Medicare program. But Medicare also retained its requirement that CRNAs be supervised by a physician (not specifically an anesthesiologist) in order for the healthcare facility to receive Medicare reimbursement. This created a bit of a Catch-22.

Because the supervision requirement was a payment issue rather than a safety or quality of care issue, it was changed in November 2001 to allow states to "opt out," which fourteen states so far have done; however, it is a lengthy process. North Carolina, like the majority of states, feels it would be desirable to bow out, but it seems content with the status quo, because to make the change would be a long, time-consuming and expensive process. The state nurse anesthetists association has also not made it a priority, explains an industry expert.

Certified Registered Nurse Anesthetists are registered nurses who have spent an additional two to three years in anesthesia training and have been certified to practice in outpatient medical facilities. In North Carolina, CRNAs are regulated by the North Carolina Board of Nursing.

In contrast, medical anesthesiologists have earned a full medical degree with a specialty in anesthesiology.

The American Association of Nurse Anesthetists (AANA) estimates that there are currently more than 37,000 nurse anesthetists nationwide, 42 percent of them male (compared to approximately 8 percent of men in nursing overall) and 58 percent female.

"CRNAs are trained to provide every type of anesthesia, in every surgical setting working in collaboration with all types of surgeons and other healthcare providers," explained a spokesperson for the AANA. "They work with the youngest and oldest of patients, and are the predominant providers of anesthesia care in the military, in rural communities, and to expectant moms."

Nurse anesthesia has always been a popular career choice for critical care nurses, but in recent years its popularity has increased considerably due to exceptional compensation and the high degree of autonomy and professional respect afforded a CRNA.

Sally Hill was not the only one who found the specialty to be a good career choice.

In a recent survey of medical professionals, when asked, "If you had it to do all over again, would you choose medicine as your career path?" many professionals would answer an emphatic "No," citing issues like the cost of malpractice insurance or the constraints of managed care.

Certified registered nurse anesthetists were the big exception. In a 2005 CRNA survey, nearly 90 percent of respondents said they would stick to medicine if they were to choose all over again.

"They enjoy the responsibility and challenge of the job and, of course, the compensation," said the company who conducted the survey.

"The aging population and the rising number of outpatient procedures requiring anesthesia care has increased the demand for these practitioners," said the AANA spokesperson. "Not surprisingly market forces have driven an increase in CRNA compensation as well."

According to the AANA the average CRNA salary in 1999 was about $102,000. Six years later, the average salary was approaching $130,000.

The criteria to become a CRNA are stringent. In 1989 a bachelor of science degree was required, but today a nurse anesthetist is required to have a master's degree. The CRNA is required to hold a current license as a registered nurse and must have at least one year of experience as a registered nurse in an acute care setting such as an ICU.

Certified Registered Nurse Anesthesia programs generally run twenty-four to thirty-six months and include clinical training in university-based and large community hospitals. All told, it takes seven to eight years of education and clinical training directly related to nursing/anesthesia to become a CRNA.

At present there were 108 nurse anesthesia programs around the country, with more than 1,700 affiliated clinical sites in the U.S. Some 2,000 new nurse anesthetists are credentialed each year. After graduation they must successfully pass a certification examination administered by the Council on Certification of Nurse Anesthetists and be recertified every two years by obtaining forty or more hours of continuing education.

Once they are employed, a nurse anesthetist will generally be required to have malpractice insurance covering $1 million per incident or a total of $3 million.

It is the responsibility of the nurse anesthetist to examine the patient before the surgery to determine if there are any potential problems with anesthetic airways and breathing. Occasionally airway problems and drug interactions happen, says a Charlotte surgeon, but generally plastic surgery patients are healthy.

It is the CRNA who determines the anesthetic plan which is generally discussed with the doctor beforehand; however, the doctor may not know all the details about the anesthetic drugs that will be used. Clearly doctors rely on the CRNA to decide on the appropriate anesthetic plan for the patient.

Under the North Carolina Nursing Act, Sally Hill and other nurse anesthetists are supposed to report directly to the doctor in charge of the facility in which they work. While the CRNA is certainly responsible for his/her actions, it is ultimately the doctor who will be held accountable.

"I've always had great respect for the profession [nurse anesthetists]; I always tell people not to worry about getting the right surgeon, they need to make sure they choose the right anesthetist," a prominent plastic surgeon said. "We always say their jobs are 'hours of boredom punctuated by sheer panic.'"

It is common knowledge in the medical profession that if something goes wrong during surgery, it will usually be the anesthetist who is blamed, regardless of who was at fault, he added.

The AANA is quick to point out that anesthesia incidents are pretty rare nowadays with 1 death in 250,000 anesthetics given. "It's one of the best medical safety records out there," says the spokesperson.

The fact that nurse anesthetists are generally compulsive about double-checking equipment and procedures, for deciding on the appropriate medications and checking a patient's vitals after surgery makes it even more difficult to understand how so many things could have gone so wrong on the day Sandra Joyner died.

"Vitals should always be monitored to make sure the oxygen level doesn't go below a set point; if it does, an alarm should sound. If it appears that a patient has been narcotized, it is general knowledge that Narcan should be given immediately to offset the overdose," the doctor explained. "It is common knowledge that too much narcotic will decrease respiratory drive."

Dr. Lee Ann McGinnis, a Presbyterian Hospital anesthesiologist, has said publicly that fentanyl is often used in office-based surgery because it works so fast. She added that the dose given would depend on the length of the surgery and the patient's metabolism. But the use of fentanyl during surgery is not in question, it is the use of the narcotic after surgery, while a patient is recovering, that raises concerns. In the case of Sandra Joyner, there is also a question about the total amount of fentanyl used for the surgery, and in recovery as a pain medication.

"Given in proper doses, it's a reasonably safe drug. People have to be aware of the side effects [and] be ready to handle them," said Sally's former supervisor John Snyder, who was head of the Presbyterian Hospital Anesthesiology Department and supervised Sally for ten years.

In a local plastic surgeon's opinion, it was not unusual for the CRNA to give medication in the recovery room without consulting the doctor. "In recovery, if the patient has discomfort, they are generally given a small amount of fentanyl or other pain medication, but of course, the amount for a one-hundred-pound person is not the same as someone who weighs two hundred pounds."

But he also pointed out that if a patient appears to be overmedicated (narcotized) they should be given Narcan right away, and the doctor should be notified immediately any time there is a change in the patient's condition.

"The point is that anyone in the anesthesia field, as soon as they see someone overnarcotized, should know to immediately give them Narcan," he added.

In his mind it all depends on the time span between the first injection of fentanyl and when Narcan was administered. It is critical to know when the patient became unable to breathe, he added.

"That's when the timing is critical," said another doctor. "That's the time when someone needs to be watching the patient very closely for any changes. The time span between the fentanyl and Narcan, when the patient was unable to breathe, is critical, especially if the patient was unattended during that time. Clearly there was an overdose of medicine in Sandra Joyner's case . . . whether it was accidental or not, is the question."

TWENTY

Cosmetic Surgery Rewards and Risks

Sandra was not unlike millions of baby boomers.

Plastic surgery can be a boon to our self-esteem as well as perk up our appearance, since we clearly live in a youth-oriented society.

By correcting these aging features, which generally occur on the bottom two-thirds of the face, by creating uplifted contours, improved facial tone and underlying muscle, a person will look more youthful and rested.

Basically a facelift should not change the fundamental appearance of a person; it should be merely restorative, it cannot stop the aging process, according to plastic surgery literature. And when the sagging is isolated to the mid-facial region where excess skin is less a factor, a mini-facelift can be done instead of a traditional facelift.

According to a brochure produced by the American Society of Plastic Surgeons, cosmetic procedures work best on adults who are healthy, non-smokers and individuals who have a positive outlook and realistic goals in mind, which Sandra apparently did.

The process typically begins with a consultation with the doctor to educate the patient about the procedure that would be best for them. At the same time there is a discussion of goals to make sure there are realistic objectives, and an overall health evaluation that includes a history, current medications, vitamins, herbs and use of alcohol, tobacco and drugs used by the patient. Techniques for facelifts are highly individualized depending on the person's particular skin, muscle and bone structure, and conditions that might contribute to their aging process such as excessive sunning.

In general, facelift incisions are made at the temple in the hairline. The skin is re-draped over the uplifted contour and the excess skin is then trimmed away. Tissues are then repositioned and mid-facial muscles are elevated to improve skin and texture. Once the incisions are healed, they will be well concealed within the hairline and the natural contours of the face and ears.

Initially there will be swelling and bruising, but the aftereffects subside within a couple of weeks. The end result is that the patient has a more youthful and rested appearance which helps them feel more confident about themselves.

During the consultation a patient generally gets instructions that will help her fully understand the procedure and any risks and potential complications. Among the risks associated with a surgical facelift are: infection; bleeding beneath the skin (hematoma); hair loss at the incision, which can be corrected; facial nerve injury with weakness; facial asymmetry; and skin loss with scarring and numbness.

After the surgery is complete a bandage is placed around the patient's face to minimize swelling and bruising. A thick tube may be present to drain any excess blood that might collect under the skin.

Before the patient is released from the medical facility the patient and an accompanying family member, friend or caregiver will be given specific instructions on how to care for the incision, medications to take or apply to help aid healing and prevent infection, and things to watch for regarding the surgical site and the patient's overall health. It is suggested that the patient follow up with the doctor after a determined period of time, generally a week.

The initial period of healing generally includes swelling and may involve numbness and discomfort that can be controlled with medication. The patient's skin will look bruised and discolored and facial movements may be temporarily restricted, but these are all common in the early stages of the healing process.

The brochure states that a patient can usually resume most activities in a few days. For the most part facelift incisions are well-healed within a week and the patient can expect to return to work and light, normal activity within 2–4 weeks. Healing is expected to continue for several more weeks as the swelling diminishes and incision lines disappear. At that point any remaining bruising or discoloration can easily be covered with cosmetics. It may take several months for all of the swelling to fully dissipate, and up to six months for the incision lines to fully mature.

Generally speaking, when something does go wrong during cosmetic surgery, it is often because of complicating factors not related to the surgery itself. The November 2007 death of Donda West, 58, mother of award-winning rapper Kanye West, after having a tummy tuck and breast reduction is one example.

Ms. West was found at home the day after her surgery, not breathing and in respiratory arrest. Shortly afterward she was pronounced dead at Centinela Freeman Regional Medical Center in Marina del Rey.

Donda's death made headlines as the media zeroed in on the doctor who had performed the surgery: Jan Adams, a celebrity surgeon who practices in Beverly Hills and has been on several TV shows, including *Plastic Surgery: Before and After* (on the Discovery Channel). He also authored *Everything Women of Color Should Know About Cosmetic Surgery.*

It was reported that Adams was not board-certified—a fact that he acknowledged on national television but discounted. It was also reported that Adams had a number of malpractice suits against him, a couple that had been settled and a couple still pending. According to reports, the California Medical Board had looked into revoking or suspending Dr. Adams's license as recently as April 2007, based on alcohol-related charges not directly related to his activities as a surgeon, but he was still licensed and practicing in November 2007.

Another plastic surgeon told the media that Donda West had initially contacted him about performing her plastic surgery, but because she had thyroid trouble he said she would have to get a medical note from her internist before he would even consider doing the surgery. In a television interview, the doctor said he had talked to West a couple of weeks prior to her surgery with Dr. Adams and she admitted that she had not gotten the medical OK.

It is not known if Dr. Adams required any type of medical note before her surgery, but Adams has insisted that he did nothing that would have caused Donda West's death.

In fact, despite questions raised about Adams by the media, the official findings appeared to reject any suggestion that Donda's cosmetic surgery was the immediate cause of her death.

"It is my opinion Ms. West died from some preexisting coronary artery disease and multiple postoperative factors following surgery," Dr. Louis A. Pena, a deputy medical examiner, stated in his autopsy report.

A spokesman for the medical examiner's office told reporters, "There was no evidence of a surgical or anesthetic misadventure. . . . The surgery itself was not the cause. It appears that she did have existing cardiac issues.

While the coroner's office said the autopsy indicated West had a blood clot in her lung veins, there was evidence of a heart attack and vomit in her breathing tubes and fluid in her lung tissue, the cause of death was inconclusive.

It was reported that Ms. West may have taken too much pain medication trying to control the pain after her procedures.

Commenting on pain control during and after cosmetic surgery, Dr. Barry Friedberg, who spoke about West's death to the media and who has coincidentally provided anesthesiology for Dr. Jan Adams on a couple of occasions, notes that narcotics like codeine or Vicodin (synthetic codeine) are commonly used to manage post-op pain. He says the worst side effect of those medications is the stoppage of breathing when too high a blood level is reached after too much pain medicine is taken.

Dr. Friedberg prefers to utilize BIS-monitored, propofol ketamine IV sedation, known as Minimally Invasive Anesthesia (MIA), which mimics general anesthesia, because it is simpler and safer. He says MIA prevents the pain of the local anesthetic from reaching the brain, which is preemptive analgesia.

Dr. Friedberg said that on rare occasions, patients having abdominoplasty with breast reduction have been admitted to a hospital for continuous intraveneous (IV) narcotic therapy to control post-op pain.

"No patient, including those having abdominoplasty and breast reduction, under MIA have needed narcotics—IV or oral—for post-op pain in ten years," he explained. "It was likely the manner in which the surgery was performed (i.e., under general anesthesia), did not reliably produce preemptive analgesia and, therefore, necessitated post-op narcotics to manage pain," he said. (More about his MIA technique and Bio monitor later.)

There are any number of stories on the Internet and in

the headlines about plastic surgeries gone wrong for one reason or another. But most everyone is convinced that death from plastic surgery can usually be avoided if appropriate procedures are followed.

It is clearly the doctor's responsibility to educate his patient about all the risks involved, to make sure the person is in good enough health for the surgery and to ensure that, where necessary, the surgery has been approved by an internist, but it is also the patient's responsibility to make sure any medical conditions she has will withstand the anesthesia and surgery.

After all, any kind of surgery has risks involved.

TWENTY-ONE

Plastic Surgery Deaths

All of the deaths due to plastic surgery don't make national headlines like Sandra Joyner's, but there have certainly been enough to cause concern.

In 2004, Olivia Goldsmith, best-selling author of *The First Wives Club* and other popular novels that often involved plastic surgery themes died in a prestigious Manhattan hospital while having minor plastic surgery, a chin tuck.

She had had several minor procedures in the past, performed by the same doctor, Norman Pastorek, a well-regarded ear, nose and throat (ENT) physician with a devoted following. To Goldsmith, the procedure was no big deal.

Goldsmith had opted for general anesthesia, which is more dangerous and not standard for the operation she was having. But because the surgery was being done in a hospital—a well-respected one—nurses were permitted to administer the anesthesia as long as they were being overseen by an anesthesiologist, who might be tending to several patients at the same time.

Goldsmith was barely on the table when she began having spasms, enormous ones. She was in distress before the surgeon even began to work on her.

Within four minutes, she was in a coma from which she never did wake up. Eight days later she was removed from life support. At the time, her family and friends asked many of the same questions as Sandra Joyner's loved ones: Was something overlooked in her history? Did they know she had suffered from depression and apprehension? Did she have an underlying disease?

Julie Rubenzer, a 5' 6", 120-pound cheerleader from the Milwaukee area was a beautiful woman. After moving to Florida, newly divorced and beginning to date, Julie decided to get her breasts enlarged at a private clinic in Sarasota. Her surgeon, Dr. Kurt Dangl, a dentist and oral surgeon by training—one of a handful of medical professions authorized to perform plastic surgery—had advertised his services on a website, complete with testimonials and the magic phrase "board-certified."

But Dr. Dangl was not certified by any board recognized by the state of Florida. And he did not have admitting privileges at any hospital. Even more worrisome: "He cut corners by not having an anesthesiologist or a nurse anesthesiologist in the room," according to one of the doctor's surgical technicians who had assisted him with dozens of surgeries.

He said Dangl often administered too much anesthesia, and "at the beginning of the procedures, many times, he had witnessed patients that would stop breathing."

Another of Dangl's patients, 64-year-old Clara Scott, had surgery that lasted for nine hours instead of the projected five. Clara's daughter was horrified when Dr. Dangl sent her mother home just half an hour after the surgery was completed.

"Her head was as big around as a basketball. And her limbs were just jerking around," her daughter said.

* * *

A death due to plastic surgery always seems to create a greater interest in the procedures and the risks involved. Then interest subsides again when everyone forgets the headlines.

The deaths of several people in 1997 due to plastic surgery prompted the selection of Dr. Barry Friedberg from over 40,000 U.S. anesthesiologists to write the first textbook in the field, *Anesthesia in Cosmetic Surgery*, which is geared to doctors. In 2001 his website, www.drfriedberg.com, was launched to help empower patients about anesthesia risks and options, and, more importantly, how to ask for safe methods.

Dr. Friedberg, who has practiced in Corona del Mar, California, since 1992, is lobbying for Minimally Invasive Anesthesia (MIA) and the use of a BIS monitor to help prevent anesthesia-related problems during cosmetic surgery.

"Minimally Invasive Anesthesia gives patients what they desire from general anesthesia—not hearing, experiencing or remembering the surgery—without the lesser trespass of sedation," he explained. General anesthesia sleep levels occur between readings of 45 and 60 units, a range where the patient doesn't hear, feel or remember the surgery, he says, but the same experience can be achieved with intravenous propofol at BIS between 60–75 units, a level Dr. Friedberg has trademarked as an integral part of MIA.

General anesthesia for cosmetic surgery, he has said, is not only unnecessary but also fraught with potentially lethal consequences, like pulmonary embolism, vomiting with aspiration and respiratory arrest secondary to postoperative narcotic pain medications.

"All of these potential complications are avoided with MIA," he has stated.

More anesthesia providers are beginning to recognize

the advantages of MIA, but surgeons and anesthesia providers need to be asked by patients to provide it to optimize safety for cosmetic surgery, he explains.

Dr. Freidberg also has some interesting perspectives on fentanyl:

"First, it is the number one drug of choice among anesthetic personnel under the age of forty with addiction problems; alcohol is the drug of choice in people over forty," he said.

"It is sneaky, unlike Demerol, because you can squirt it into coffee or a can of soda. More importantly, it can be easily disguised in urine by taking a Valium by mouth."

In his opinion there is massive ignorance about fentanyl and the risks involved.

According to *The New York Times*, Dr. Benjamin N. Riger, chairman of the anesthesiology department at the University of Louisville School of Medicine said he has seen six colleagues in fifteen years become addicted to fentanyl or sufentanil, a similar drug that is even more powerful.

"When users become addicted, which can occur rapidly—sometimes after only a few injections—they feel an intense craving, accompanied by anxiety and insomnia, to return to the euphoria of the high," said Dr. William P. Arnold III, chairman of the committee of the American Society of Anesthesiologists, which is collecting information on fentanyl addiction. "If I was being operated on and I knew the surgeon was addicted to fentanyl," he said, "I would pray that he had some on board during the operation, just to smooth him out."

Although he wasn't involved in Sandra Joyner's case, Dr. Friedberg did have a similar one at a hospital in Newport Beach, California.

"A patient was in a holding area waiting to be picked

up by a relative when a technician gave the patient fentanyl in an IV without documenting it or telling anyone before he left. The next person came along and gave them another dose, and the patient died.

He says this is a common theme in fentanyl overdoses—they happen when people aren't paying attention and don't document how much fentanyl has been given and when.

"Subsequently it's very difficult to prove," Friedberg says. Suppose Sandra Joyner was given 5 ccs of fentanyl during surgery and then two more in recovery. Then, he says, "She was lucky she survived five ccs in surgery. Adding two more ccs in the recovery room would be like lighting a match to gasoline. Fentanyl is supposed to be used for the short term. But when it is given at eight a.m. for surgery, then in the recovery room, it has become long-acting, which is the risk. It isn't metabolized quickly," he added.

Dr. Freidberg began looking into safer ways to dispense anesthesia because of the number of avoidable deaths from fentanyl from 1995 to1997.

"There is no reason why patients have to suffer increased risks when undergoing anesthesia. We should use the most intelligent way, so the patient will not have side effects. We should be able to put them to sleep without side effects," he adds.

For the past ten years, Dr. Friedberg has been using a BIS monitor, which automatically tracks a patient's breath, respiration, etc., instead of the anesthetist gauging it on his/her own while the patient is under anesthesia. Malpractice carriers have been endorsing the product, which he has no stake in, other than his belief that it is an added measure against complications and death, which he talks about in *Anesthesia in Cosmetic Surgery*.

But he also says that some doctors and anesthetists are resistant. They "have attitude," and it's difficult to get them to change the way they have been doing things.

In the book he recommends the MIA technique and the BIS monitor. He also suggests that the anesthesiologist develop a close working relationship with the surgeon and that patients be careful when they are having extensive and often lengthy procedures.

His website was designed to help educate patients about anesthesia so they can become involved in the process as well.

TWENTY-TWO

Accident vs. Murder

One of Sally's classmates has said, "She didn't do enough to help her patient," referring to Sally not going into emergency procedures when Sandra was clearly in trouble, but Sally's friends and most of her Olympic High classmates just don't believe she would have intentionally murdered Sandra; if anything, they believe it would have been an accident.

The medical community points out that accidents do happen, and they believe the public might be too quick to rush to a judgment of murder.

An online nursing journal ran a story about a nurse who had attached the wrong IV bag, causing the patient to die. The nurse was charged with murder. The medical journal asked the question "When Does Malpractice Become Murder?"

An American Medical Association online magazine also discussed the issue in an article headlined "Malpractice or Murder? Criminalization of medical errors is a troubling trend."

The article, written by Tanya Albert (10/10 for AMNews), said physicians traditionally worry about malpractice lawsuits and license suspensions resulting from their medical decisions. Now there's an added fear of landing in criminal court or possibly jail. She wrote:

> When physicians picked up newspapers a decade ago and read about a colleague charged with a crime, it was most often a crime that had nothing to do with medical decision-making. Today that's not always the case.
>
> Increasingly, doctors and nurses are being charged with crimes as a result of medical decisions made in the operating room, emergency department or office exam room.
>
> "Things have changed," said Kansas surgeon and lawyer Thomas R. McLean, MD, a physician attorney who teaches at the University of Missouri-Kansas City and University of Kansas schools of medicine. "As a doctor, I can go to jail for a medical error." He has been researching the criminalization of medical errors.
>
> Over the past couple of years, doctors have been charged with murder for prescribing pain medicine. But they've also been prosecuted for underprescribing for pain. A state prosecutor accused one physician of treating wounds in a way that violated laws designed to protect the elderly. Doctors also have faced criminal and civil charges for the way they've billed Medicare and Medicaid. . . .
>
> "There's been a small but a clearly disturbing number of cases where a doctor is charged with a crime," said American Medical Association President Richard F. Corlin, MD.

Medical and legal experts are quick to point out that the number of physicians who have been charged with

crimes is relatively small, and the chances of an overzeal-
ous prosecutor pressing charges remain remote.

The same is true of nurses.

A Wisconsin case that criminally charged a nurse after
an error is the latest in a trend that could drive doctors and
nurses away from the practice of medicine or that inter-
fere with patient treatment and safety.

On November 2, 2007, the Wisconsin attorney general
charged Julie Thao, RN, with criminal negligence after a
July 2006 incident where the wrong medication was fa-
tally administered to 16-year-old Jasmine Gant.

Wisconsin physicians and hospital leaders agreed
that the event was an unintentional mistake. But the
state's complaint said that Thao's "failure to provide adequate medical care and gross breach of medical protocol created a significant danger and caused great bodily
harm to Jasmine Gant." In the end, Thao's nursing license was suspended for nine months, she received pro-
bation and St. Mary's Hospital settled with the family
for $1.9 million. However, several nursing associations
and the Wisconsin Hospital Association have opposed
criminal prosecution of health workers for "unintentional
errors" and legislation is being drafted to prevent it in
the future.

Medical and legal experts say this type of case is extremely rare and possibly unprecedented in the state. But
it was the third Wisconsin case in four months involving
criminal proceedings against medical professionals.

In Illinois an emergency department may be charged
with involuntary manslaughter after a heart attack patient
died after waiting two hours to be treated.

A consultant anesthestist who twice accidentally injected
air into a 6-week-old baby's bloodstream during routine
stomach surgery called on the physician immediately, but

the baby died anyway. The anesthetist was cleared of any wrongdoing.

A 10-year-old boy died after he failed to come off anesthesia following a routine tooth extraction. According to reports, the anesthetist was being investigated.

When an ear, nose and throat specialist prematurely was alleged to have removed a breathing tube that was keeping open the patient's airway after surgery, the dentist was charged criminally because he had failed to review the patient's notes about breathing difficulties. The patient later went to the hospital, where she suffered respiratory arrest and anoxic brain injury.

Another example of how claims of malpractice and murder overlap involves the death of an 8-year-old boy after the anesthesiologist allegedly fell asleep during the child's surgery and the boy died. Also, three nurses were charged criminally for a neonate's death after the baby was given an overdose of penicillin.

Doctors worry that a threat of being charged with a crime for a medical error, or for something they did while trying their best to treat a patient, will affect treatment decisions and hinder improvements in care.

Medical malpractice in itself is complicated. "By its very definition, malpractice means negligence—a deviation from an expected duty of care. Murder is a criminal act involving the intent to commit a crime," explained Fred W. DeVore III, a Charlotte attorney who specializes in medical malpractice cases.

"Therefore, in nearly every case, the terms 'malpractice' and 'murder' are mutually exclusive. If you intend to commit a crime, it's not negligence, it is more like a mistake (there are rare exceptions). I've never seen malpractice characterized as murder."

In general, "medical malpractice" occurs when a medical provider (a doctor or hospital) makes a mistake and "breaches the standard of care."

"However, a doctor (or nurse) can be charged with a crime if he is grossly negligent, operating drunk or after his license was suspended, for example," said DeVore.

Most attorneys consider medical malpractice cases extremely complex, and require testimony from medical experts. Often physicians, hospitals and insurance companies have access to information, experts and defense funds that patients and their families do not.

"Doctors (and nurses) are already paranoid about attorneys and lawsuits. I believe it would be a terrible mischaracterization to say that a doctor (or nurse) who commits malpractice, even if it results in the death of a patient, is subject to criminal charges. Such a case is extremely rare with extenuating circumstances," he added.

In the case of Sandra Joyner's death and the subsequent murder charges against Sally Hill, DeVore says, "Intent is hard to prove in a case like this. We don't know what evidence they have—unless she confessed, told someone she was going to do it, or deliberately tampered with the medication."

According to statistics provided by the National Practitioner Data Bank:

— 3,009 medical malpractice reports regarding registered nurses were made to the National Practitioner Databank in the U.S. 1990–2004
— 16,339 nurses and nursing-related practitioners had a malpractice report made against them in the U.S. 1990–2003.

But none seems to be as serious as the charges against Sally Hill.

TWENTY-THREE

Who Would Kill a Patient?

It is hard to believe that anyone who has taken an oath to care for the sick would ever deliberately do anything to harm the patient they are caring for.

Yet, history is full of cases where medical professionals have intentionally killed a patient, even a series of patients under their care, like a serial killer.

Is there a psychological profile of a medical killer? It is generally known that there is usually some type of a relationship between the victim and the offender, and while motivation is not apparent, it is certainly shrouded. Rarely is the murder about money—the medical professional usually does it for the thrill and/or dominance they achieve in their own world.

In the case of serial killers in the medical profession—like Angel of Mercy killers who think they are putting a patient out of his or her misery—profilers usually tend to look back at the person's childhood: dysfunctional backgrounds involving sexual or physical abuse, drugs or alcoholism and their related problems, disorganized thinking, bipolar mood disorders, resentment toward society and an inability to be social or socially accepted; or they may also have overbearing parents. If they feel isolated and have a wild imagination, they drift into a fantasy world that includes daydreaming.

The isolation in turn can breed ideation of inadequacy and feelings of not being good enough. These feelings are masked by numerous artificial successes, but the feelings run deeper than the normal neurotic feelings of not being good enough. These early feelings are known as "bonding," which set up a map of how the child will react to others later in life.

Several therapists say that murderers see themselves as dominant, controlling and powerful figures. They hold the power of life and death, and in their own eyes, they perceive themselves as God. This may be the only power they have ever had, says author B. F. Skinner in his book *Science and Human Behavior*.

Serial killers can believe that they have fallen into the power of the devil after several kills, which is contrary to their initial belief that they were God.

The F.B.I. has a list of personality traits that identify such killers: social withdrawal, abnormal dependence on or ulcerated relations with one's parents, hypochondria or other attention-seeking behavior including a delusional mind, feelings of grandeur, severe depression, a general feeling of emptiness toward the future, inability to take criticism, a general feeling of being mistreated, inability to assert oneself, parental taunts as to one's inability to be sufficient, mood disorders and a general failing in attempts to succeed.

In most cases there is a "pre-crime stressor"—a reason the person turned to murder for a release. There are also sociopaths, someone with a disorder of character rather than of the mind. Sociopaths lack a conscience, feel no remorse and care exclusively for their own pleasures in life.

For instance: In the early morning hours of January 13,

2004, on the eve of his 58th birthday, Harold Shipman, one of the most prolific serial killers of our time, was found hanged in his cell at Wakefield Prison. Born in Nottingham, England, Shipman was found guilty of murdering fifteen people in 2000 and sentenced to fifteen concurrent life sentences.

What made these tragic crimes so heinous in the eyes of the world was that Harold Shipman was not your everyday average sociopath—he was a medical doctor, sworn by oath to "do no harm."

It is unclear how many patients Dr. Shipman actually murdered, but it is estimated the number was around 250, 80 percent of whom were women, the youngest of which was only 41 years old.

He was well-respected in the community and had a wife and children, plus a flourishing medical career, but somehow he ended up on the dark side of medicine.

As far back as the 1800s Dr. Henry H. Holmes (1860–1896) trapped and reportedly murdered hundreds of guests at his Chicago hotel, which opened in 1893 for the World's Columbian Exhibition. It became known as the Castle of Death because he had piped in special gas lines so he could asphyxiate guests. Some victims were locked away in a gigantic bank vault close to his office where he could hear their screams until they suffocated. Later he put them down a secret chute to the basement where they would be made into "skeleton models." He would then sell them to the medical schools, for a profit.

The death toll was said to be around 230. Only twenty-seven, however, were verified by police. In May 1896, Dr. Holmes was hanged for his brutal crimes. Even then he remained calm and collected, telling a prison guard that he "never slept better in his life" on the eve of his execution.

In the 1950s John Bodkin Adams, a British general

practitioner, was suspected in the deaths of more than 160 patients, who all seemed to die under "suspicious" circumstances. In 1957 he was arrested and tried for the murder of Mrs. Edith Morrell, a wealthy widow he had cared for. He was accused of giving her lethal doses of barbiturates, morphine, and heroin. He claimed she'd died November 13, 1950, of a stroke.

He arranged for her cremation the next day. It was later learned that he had obtained a small amount of money from her estate, a Rolls-Royce Silver Ghost and an antique chest full of silverware. It was believed he visited her over 300 times during the course of her treatment and billed her estate for over 1,000 visits. In April 1957 he was acquitted of her murder.

Gertrude Hullet also fell victim to Dr. Adams when two times the lethal dose of barbiturates was found in her urine after her death in July 1956. Dr. Adams had been aware of her depression after the death of her husband and prescribed massive doses of barbiturates to ease her sorrow. Reportedly Hullet left the doctor her Rolls-Royce Silver Dawn, which he sold several days later but was never found to be criminally negligent.

During the investigation, from 1939 to 1956, ten suspicious deaths with similar circumstances occurred in patients under his care. However, he was never convicted of a single murder, although he was found to have benefited from 132 patients' wills. He was convicted of other crimes such as forging prescriptions and making false statements on cremation forms. He died in July 1983 due to complications from a hip fracture.

In San Antonio, Texas, Genene Jones, who worked for several medical clinics, and was supposed to care for innocent children in the community, instead brutally murdered them. It is thought she killed between eleven and forty-six infants and children between 1980 and

1982 using lethal injections of insulin and succinyl-choline to kill the children.

There may have been more, but it was claimed that Texas hospital officials may have destroyed all of her employment records to prevent further embarrassment or trials. She was charged with two counts of murder and is currently serving 99 years in prison. Because of a law in Texas that prevents overcrowding of jails, she will only have to serve one-third of her sentence. She will be automatically paroled in 2017.

One of the most recent cases of an Angel of Death is Charles Cullen. In 2003 he confessed to killing forty-five patients over the preceding sixteen years at ten different New Jersey and Pennsylvania hospitals where he had worked with insulin and digoxin. Hospital officials got suspicious when Cullen was found accessing records of patients not assigned to him. He also requested medication that was not prescribed for patients.

Cullen said he wanted to end their suffering and prevent the hospital from "dehumanizing" them. He is currently serving eighteen consecutive life sentences, and won't be eligible for parole for 397 years.

The question is: What would cause these medical professionals to commit such heinous acts?

In a study done by F.B.I. psychological criminologist Robert Ressler in the late 1970s, the answers seemed to take on a disturbing metamorphosis.

It was based on interviews with thirty-six incarcerated murderers who shared similar traits and backgrounds. Behavioral traits that were found to be commonplace among them included a severely dysfunctional family background involving mental illness, alcohol and drug abuse, and actual criminal behavior of the parents themselves.

Each murderer interviewed reported to have suffered severe emotional abuse as a child. It was also discovered that each had a critical, domineering mother figure who deprived them of love and emotional support, and sometimes an absent father.

When the implicit trust relationship between doctors and nurses and the patients they care for is exploited for their own, perverse, deviant gain, it chips away at the fundamental core of our society, weakening social mores and values in a way that is often beyond repair, author Deborah Trendel, RN, BSN, PHN, claimed in her article "The Dark Side of Medicine: Doctors and Nurses Who Kill," published on About.com.

There wasn't anything in Sally's history that would indicate a predisposition to murder a patient. The only possible reason for such an act, as the police believe, is if she had been holding a grudge for thirty years. Proof of that would be almost impossible to substantiate.

Olympic High School classmate Ronnie Stack is adamant that Sally wouldn't and couldn't have deliberately killed Sandra Baker Joyner: "I know in my heart she wouldn't have done that. If you ask me, she's a scapegoat. The facts will speak for themselves.

"When it's all said and done, and she's not found guilty, there will be plenty of attorneys who want to help her file a lawsuit."

TWENTY-FOUR

Foolproofing the System

Clients almost always check the reputation of a surgeon (although everything doesn't make it into the public record), but it is difficult, if not impossible, to determine how well an office handles an emergency, for instance. But that's not to say that if office procedures are sloppy or a medical professional has a sketchy past, a patient would never know.

Recently a New Jersey newspaper reported on an anesthesiologist who was convicted of manslaughter in England in February 2001, after failing to monitor a patient under his care. Unable to practice in England, the physician came back to the States and renewed his New Jersey license by allegedly checking "no" when asked if he had been convicted of a crime, and whether his license had been suspended or revoked.

Since he was a foreigner, the conviction was not recorded on the National Practitioner Data Bank. Even when the conviction was reported to the state board, it took eleven months for a complaint to be filed. He was allowed to practice while he was under investigation and during the appeal process.

In 2002 the New Jersey Board of Nursing disciplined fifty-six nurses and another sixty-eight had their nursing licenses revoked or voluntarily surrendered them. State nursing boards want to raise awareness of what should be reported and the National Council of State Boards of Nursing (NCSBN) is coordinating the boards in a national system, the Nurse Data Bank, to allow better access to complaints and records across state lines. Twenty-seven nursing boards now participate.

When Charles Cullen admitted to killing thirty to forty patients during his fourteen-year career it got everyone's attention. One of the most dramatic elements was his employment record. Ten times he had been hired, five times fired, four times questioned about patients' deaths and twice accused of improper administration of medications. The system had allowed him to move from one healthcare facility to another without suspicions, without alarm, without raising an eyebrow.

It was his record and abuse of it that ripped open the shocking flaw in the nation's system of screening healthcare professionals. Lawmakers were among the first to react, expressing the need for better systems and comprehensive databases that would mandate more inclusive reporting of healthcare professionals.

Currently physician data is compiled within two systems: The National Practitioner Data Bank (NPBD) created by Congress in 1990 and the Federation of State Medical Boards (FSMB), a centralized database that compiles reports from each of the individual state medical boards.

However, experts say that does not make them foolproof.

"We need to look at how we can strengthen the reporting requirements," Cheryl Peterson, RN, of the American Nurses Association, has said. "We need to bring all healthcare practitioners up to the same standard of care that is used for physicians."

Bruce Sackman, special agent in charge of the Office

of the Inspector General, Northeast Field Office, U.S. Department of Veteran Affairs (VA) has a great respect for the role that nurses can play in the investigation of suspicious deaths. He worked on the investigations of two notable healthcare serial killers, and credits nurses' attention to detail with breaking the cases.

"Healthcare facilities need to develop policies and procedures regarding suspicious deaths," Sackman says. "Management has to establish a standard operating procedure so staff knows what to do when they have suspicions. Just as facilities have disaster drills, suspicious-death drills must be incorporated into their regular training. They must know how to secure evidence and protect the crime scene."

He also says whistle-blowers should be protected, and there must be immunity for facilities that report suspicious activity. Every licensed healthcare provider ought to have the authorization to declare suspicious deaths, and know how to inaugurate an investigation. And every hospital should have a forensic nurse on staff, he added. "I think that every hospital should have a forensic nurse, a trained staff person who can work with police to conduct suspicious death investigations," Sackman said. "The nurse is able to bridge the gap, translating all of that medical information and hospital routine for law enforcement investigators. I would not do a healthcare investigation without a nurse on my team."

TWENTY-FIVE

The Investigation

In 2001 Sandra Joyner's death was ruled an accident. It was tragic for everyone involved and especially hard on her sons Grayson and Philip.

Sandra wouldn't see them grow into young men, get married and have families of their own; their children would not know their grandmother.

The boys' father, who had been estranged from Sandra at the time of her death, was consumed with guilt. If they not been separated, if they had still been married, and she hadn't been trying to establish a new life and get a job, would her appearance have been so important? Could Sandra and John eventually have reconciled, as he had hoped, and once again been a happy family?

Unfortunately John Joyner would have to ponder those questions for the rest of his life.

Sandra's death touched everyone who came in contact with her that day. Dr. Tucker had to be concerned whether his plastic surgery practice would survive the negative publicity.

Sally was fired by Dr. Tucker a month after Sandra died. Her nursing license was revoked, the career she had worked so hard for was over and her leukemia flared up again. She also felt responsible for Sandra's death.

If she did not have her faith, she told friends, she didn't know how she would have survived the tragedy.

It had been a slow healing process for all of them.

Then, out of nowhere, early in January 2006, Detective Chuck Henson, a Charlotte–Mecklenburg Police Department cold case detective, got a request from his supervisor to reopen the case.

New information, an anonymous tip, had come to the district attorney's attention five years after Sandra's death. It raised questions about foul play, and the district attorney believed a closer look at the case was warranted.

Detective Henson had been a Homicide detective for six years, the last two of them working cold cases. A good portion of them tended to go nowhere, and he wasn't sure this one would be any different.

"I didn't really think I would find anything new, I thought it would be another routine investigation," he recalled.

But he was dead wrong.

He began the process by talking to everyone involved in the case from Dr. Tucker and Sally's co-workers, to the paramedics, and Sandra and Sally's friends from high school.

Of particular interest to Detective Henson was the comment Sally had made during Sandra's 1999 procedure, which had not been brought up during the medical board or nursing board investigations.

"That's the woman that stole my boyfriend," Sally had said, having no idea it would come back to haunt her years later. It was hard to find an explanation for why Sally would even mention it thirty years after the fact.

That remark and a claim that the girls had never gotten along were disclosed to the detective and *The Charlotte Observer* by an anonymous person supposedly close to the situation, who has been deemed credible. This person helped build the theory of a thirty-year grudge.

According to the anonymous source, "the girls never got along" and "a feud had been brewing for years." The comments, in combination with other information, had never before been made public, but gave the investigation new life.

Had Sally Hill been harboring a grudge against Sandra for three decades for stealing her boyfriend in high school?

Those close to Sally thought the idea of a thirty-year grudge was ridiculous.

"It's stupid. She's not the kind of person to hold a grudge, certainly not for thirty years," said Sally's mother-in-law Anita Hill. She puts absolutely no stock in the charges. "Five years is a long time for them to come up with this now. It's the most ridiculous thing I've ever heard that she would hold a grudge for thirty years. She's not a vindictive person, never has been."

Sally's co-workers and friends agreed.

"Even if she made the comment that Sandra took her boyfriend, that certainly doesn't mean she would harm her for it," explained Patty Campbell, a circulating nurse who worked at Dr. Tucker's office along with Sally.

Detective Henson talked to Patty early on in his investigation and specifically asked if she had heard the comment that Dr. Tucker and the technician said Sally had made in 1999. Patty had no knowledge of it.

In an interview with *The Charlotte Observer*, Patty defended her co-worker, saying she believed Sandra's death was accidental. If the "boyfriend" comment had been made, Patty believed, police were making far too much of it.

"She is wrongly accused," Patty told a reporter. "Sally

doesn't have a mean bone in her body. She's my friend and I believe in her. We all say stupid things."

Still, someone had given the detective and newspaper what was considered to be evidence that Sally and Sandra never got along, that a feud had been brewing for years. What, if anything, that person knows for sure, like so many unanswered questions, will probably not surface until Sally goes to trial.

High school friends who were close to Sandra have gone on record saying that they were not even aware that the two girls knew each other, and that Sandra and Sally certainly hadn't been in touch since high school.

There wasn't any question about who the "boyfriend" was; everyone knew it was the adorable, funny boy all the girls in the high school loved—Jimmy Niell, the "hottie" with the dark hair and cocky smile who'd played football and wrestled on the high school team with John Joyner.

Dennis Poston, of Annapolis, Maryland, who dated Sally in high school in the 9th and 10th grades, says, "I do remember that Jimmy hung out with Sally for a while and then dropped her to date Sandra, but that was before Sandra and John started dating."

However, Jimmy Niell says, "I didn't really ever date Sally. I would hang out and talk to her, I went over to her apartment once, I think, but we never went anywhere together," he explained. Jimmy has said he didn't really "hang around" with Sally more than a couple of weeks, and that the time they did spend together was mostly talking and kidding around. "I didn't have my driver's license yet, so I think I got a friend to drop me off at the apartment where she lived with her mother, I think."

In contrast, he vividly recalls the time he spent with Sandra. "Sandra and I dated for a year and a half— through the tenth grade and part of the eleventh.

"She was sweet, very outgoing, she had great parents. Her sister, who was two years older than Sandra, was beautiful, too. I had a sister two years older than me, too, our sisters were in the same class together."

He remembers the Bakers being a great family "the kind of family you don't see anymore." Her father was a Navy man and "pretty strict. Her mom was as sweet as she could be. They had a good family situation," he added.

Many of the kids had gone through elementary and junior high together, he pointed out, but Jimmy had gone to Wilson Junior High, close to the airport, a good distance from where the others lived. He'd had to make all new friends. By the middle of the 11th grade, the relationship between Sandra and Jimmy was beginning to wind down.

"We didn't have a fight, there wasn't any big blowup, it had just run its course."

Or maybe he'd sensed that she had a new interest.

"She and John had lockers right next to each other, that's how they started talking to each other," he recalls.

There were no hard feelings when John, a friend and fellow wrestler on the school team, started dating Sandra and then became involved.

"There wasn't any animosity, we were winding up, we were just going our separate ways and I was happy that she and John liked each other. . . . They eventually married."

After high school he didn't see much of Sandra and John.

"I would run into John occasionally," added Jimmy, who married but later divorced his high school sweetheart Robin. Jimmy had two sons from a second marriage, which also ended in divorce.

After high school Jimmy got a business degree from the University of North Carolina at Charlotte and worked in the insurance field for most of his life. Ironically when John's company Dickerson Group, Inc., had a catastrophic fire, Jimmy was the adjuster who handled his claim.

In 2000 Jimmy took a job running a printing press for his high school friend Gregg Pence, who owns a marketing firm, a change that allowed him to spend more time with his youngest son, who was in high school. The older son was already in college.

When the story of Sandra Joyner's death, and the fact that Sally Hill had been the nurse anesthetist, made headlines, Jimmy, like so many other schoolmates, grabbed his Olympic High School yearbook to refresh his memory.

"On one of the pages Sandra wrote about how we met. She said a mutual friend had kind of shoved us together, but I didn't really remember that part," Jimmy said. He wouldn't agree to share the message she wrote in his yearbook, for fear it would upset her parents.

"I went back and looked at Sally. She was a cute blonde with pretty blue eyes," he recalled after looking through the yearbook. Then he found a photo of Sandra taken when he was playing football and she was a cheerleader. "Looking back at her in her cheerleading outfit brought back a flood of memories," he said wistfully.

The detective sat down with Sandra's parents, her sister and her estranged husband. He talked to the doctor and medical staff at the Center for Cosmetic and Plastic Surgery and several high school classmates who knew both women. He even tracked down the mysterious "boyfriend"—not John Joyner—who was thought to be at the core of the thirty-year grudge theory.

One day about seven months into the investigation, Jimmy got a telephone call at work. He was handed a message asking him to call a Detective Chuck Henson.

"I had never heard of him," Jimmy recalled.

Jimmy dialed the number and Detective Henson answered, "Homicide."

"I said, 'Whoa.' That was my first knowledge of anything."

Jimmy believes Detective Henson made the connection to him when Debbie, Sandra's sister, found out he was working for Gregg Pence.

"She probably told the detective there were only two guys that Sandra had dated seriously in high school. I was the only one other than John . . . do the math, there's only two people who dated her," he repeated.

Detective Henson told Jimmy that he had re-opened the investigation into Sandra's death and said he understood that Jimmy had dated both women in high school.

"I told him I just saw Sally very briefly, just a couple of weeks. I said I didn't consider myself a boyfriend to Sally. I wasn't around her that much, honestly. I didn't even remember going anywhere with her, like on a date."

The only thing he could remember was going to Sally's apartment one time, where he thought she lived with her mom.

"I had someone drop me off at her house, that's all I remember," he told the detective. "I think it was maybe around my birthday in March."

Right after that he started dating Sandra.

"But I was never aware of any animosity between the two girls," he added.

When Detective Henson asked him about breaking up with Sally in order to date Sandra, Jimmy says he'd told the detective emphatically, "It wasn't a situation like that. I didn't consider us girlfriend and boyfriend."

While Jimmy never considered that he and Sally were an item, it is not clear what Sally thought about their relationship. The fact that she'd even brought it up thirty years

later caused many, including Detective Henson, to believe
the brief time they'd spent "hanging out" may have been
far more important to Sally than it was to Jimmy. It
wouldn't be the first time a young girl thought, or imagined, that "hanging out" meant far more than a teenage
boy did.

Jimmy wondered what he was in for as the person at
the heart of the grudge theory. He asked Detective Henson not to give his name to the media, a request the detective honored. Henson said only that he had "talked to the
boyfriend in question," without giving his name.

"It was front-page news in *The Charlotte Observer*, and
made headlines on the evening news every day for weeks,"
Jimmy said. "I didn't want the press hounding my eighty-
year-old parents."

But Jimmy, now bald with a Fu Manchu mustache,
didn't seem to mind when a story in *People* magazine,
which also didn't name him, referred to him as a "handsome jock."

"Some of us age better than others," he said, his
charming wit still intact.

A couple of months before Sally was charged with
first-degree murder, Jimmy talked to Detective Henson
again.

"I wasn't surprised, from everything I had seen and
heard in the news, that Sally would be charged. I felt sure
she would be, after talking to Detective Henson," he recalled.

Although Jimmy hadn't seen much of John since high
school, a bond has always remained. He wanted to pay his
respects at Sandra's funeral.

"I spent a lot of time talking to him at the visitation
the night before Sandra's funeral. We're still very good
friends," he added.

As the months ticked by, the pieces of the puzzle

seemed to come together for Detective Henson. The more he learned about the two women—the supposed high school rivalry, the contrast in their lives—the more he felt that Sally had, indeed, intended to kill Sandra Joyner the day of her plastic surgery.

"You just never know what people will do if they snap," he said thoughtfully.

In a sworn deposition, Dr. Tucker told a medical board investigator that he knew the women were acquaintances, even alluded to the fact that Sandra might have said something that made Sally snap, but he didn't elaborate on what he thought that might be, according to *The Charlotte Observer*. One can only assume it would be a remark about the boyfriend Sally thought Sandra had stolen.

On September 8, 2006, eight months after Detective Henson had begun his investigation, Sally Jordan Hill was arrested and charged with first-degree murder in the death of Sandra Joyner.

That night, the nurse anesthetist who had practiced for twenty years, who had never even had a medical infraction or committed any type of crime as far as anyone knew, would spend her first night of many behind bars.

The community was shocked, especially the people who had known the two women in high school.

"I heard about it when everyone else did," said John, who was shaken by the news and has remained reticent to discuss anything about the case.

John had worked hard to put Sandra's death behind him and to heal the family after their separation and her death. For a while he threw himself into his work; he traveled a great deal and had several homes in different areas, from the Florida Keys to New York.

Eventually he decided he needed some balance in life and began to date, thinking he might like to remarry someday.

The boys, who had started college, continued to stay at the family home when in town, and John purchased an upscale penthouse where he sometimes threw parties, including a fundraiser for Pat McCrory, who is currently Charlotte's mayor and is running for governor of North Carolina.

When in town, John, who is trim and good-looking, is a familiar face at the local haunts that attract the "in crowd."

Sally's arrest for the murder of Sandra was the last thing he needed. It seemed to bring up guilt and raw emotions for him and his sons, who were trying to focus on college and their futures, but were still grieving the loss of their mother, especially the oldest son, Grayson.

John was shocked when Detective Henson showed up at the front door to tell him there had been a homicide investigation into his wife's death, and Sally's arrest was imminent.

"I'm pretty shut down now; it's a very complicated matter that could involve someone's life," John said, referring to the turn of events, adding that he didn't feel comfortable talking about it.

On September 8, the day Sally Hill was arrested, Detective Henson issued a press release explaining, without going into too much detail, that Sandra Joyner's surgery had gone well and nothing unusual had occurred.

"After her surgery, she was awake and talking," he said. "She was wheeled into the adjoining recovery room, where she was monitored by the Certified Registered Nurse Anesthetist, Sally Jordan Hill. After a brief period in the recovery room, Ms. Joyner became unresponsive and went into respiratory arrest." On April 15, 2001, the release said, "Ms. Joyner died as a result of Probable Medication Toxicity."

The release went on to say that on September 8, 2006, members of the Charlotte–Mecklenburg Police Department Cold Case Unit had arrested Sally Jordan Hill and charged her with the murder of Sandra Baker Joyner.

In closing, it mentioned that Sandra's family did not wish to comment at this time.

It was also noted that this was the twenty-first case cleared by the Homicide Cold Case Unit.

Detective Henson refused to discuss the girls' friendship, saying that to do so might speak to motive.

He was playing that very close to the vest.

TWENTY-SIX

Jail

Around 1 p.m., Detective Henson and his partner pulled into the underground parking area and escorted Sally into the jail where she would be processed. Her personal information had already been phoned in by the detective, so the paperwork—two sheets of medical information and various other forms—were waiting for her, along with a temporary wristband that would identify her while she was incarcerated.

She was still wearing a cast on her arm after wrist surgery, so they couldn't put handcuffs on her. She was also wearing a neoprene surgical boot after having a pin put in her right foot, She had thought it would be easier to have both procedures done at once. Sally was walking slowly with a slight limp as she made her way into the processing center and pre-trial detention facility at the Mecklenburg County Jail at 801 East Fourth Street, which had opened in February 1997.

One of the officers motioned for the detention nurse, who was located in a small office with a window that was off to the side of the entrance so that the nurse could inquire about Sally's foot surgery, which was standard procedure if a potential inmate had a medical condition. In fact, the nurse is required to give a medical clearance before anyone with a medical problem can be accepted into custody.

Sally was required to turn over all of her personal belongings, including any money and jewelry she had on her, so that it could be documented and stored until her release. Then she was patted down to make sure she had nothing else on her person.

Detective Henson accompanied Sally around the corner, where she was fingerprinted using a touch-screen scanner. She also underwent an iris scan to ensure that the right person was being admitted to the jail, then the information was put into a statewide computer system.

When Sally was set to have her photo taken, a guard told her, "Take the clip out of your hair." She complied, running her fingers through her blonde locks, which then fell to her shoulders. She was numb by then. "I sat in a room for an hour. They offered me some Bojangles chicken and a Coke, but I didn't take it." She later wished she had—she didn't eat until hours later and only got a baloney sandwich, chips, and an orange.

Sally was now officially an inmate instead of an arrestee. She was escorted to the first floor, where she traded in her clothing for a red jumpsuit. It was there that she was issued a permanent wristband with her photo.

Her clothes were placed in a canvas-type bag with her photo in a plastic pocket for identification. It would be stored until she was released, when it would be given back to her with her belongings.

Sally was told to take a plastic bin from the stack on the floor. It contained two sheets, a blanket and a couple of towels and washcloths. She was also issued a hygiene kit with items like a toothbrush, toothpaste, soap and shampoo. If she ran out of toiletries, she could request another kit.

From there Sally was escorted to the 4th floor, where

the women's pods, or cells, were located. At no time while incarcerated would male and female prisoners be in the same area together. On average, the jail generally has 200 women, about 1,700 men—capacity is 1,904. Along the hallway to the pod area were classrooms where inmates could receive instruction in parenting and life skills. There were also special visitation rooms where Sally and the other inmates could talk to visitors through a glass wall via telephone, though they are not very private.

A few feet down the hall were rooms that provided more privacy, where inmates could meet with their attorneys.

Inmates were allowed to have visitors—two adults or one adult and two children—for a thirty-minute visit once a week. The day for visitation depended on their pod number.

Sally would get three meals a day. Breakfast included eggs, grits and toast, and arrived at 4:30 a.m. A loud-speaker would announce the arrival of the food trays on the floor so that the inmates could line up in the hall for them.

They returned to their pods to eat their meals. For lunch they generally had a box lunch which included a sandwich and some fruit. Dinner was a hot meal, maybe chicken and mashed potatoes and a vegetable.

"If they want coffee or anything else, they have to get it from the commissary," said Sergeant Charles Pearson. Inmates could use touch screens in the pod area to order what they wanted, and it would be brought up to the floor. "They can get snacks, toiletries, underwear if they need something," he added.

There was a nice library where inmates could choose books by turning in a written request. Later in the day the books would be delivered to the inmates. There is also a law library they have access to.

The inmates' pods were aptly named, because they are only about 12' × 18'. The pod has a cot-sized bed, sink and toilet with a small bin for personal items on one side, and a small stainless-steel writing desk with a child-sized chair on the other.

A medium wattage light had to be left on at all times—even at night—so that the guards could see into the pod.

A row of showers with curtains lined one wall of the common area.

"Showering with a plastic bag on my foot—with no way to tie it shut—was a nightmare. You couldn't leave your room if you didn't shower," she explained. "They were having an outbreak of MRSA—it's a miracle I didn't lose my foot."

Inmates could use the day room in the center of the pods, where there was a community television set, and tables and stools bolted to the floor, for playing board games. They could watch any television shows they wanted—including the news—except MTV and the other music video stations.

Lockdown was 11 p.m., when everyone had to be in their pod for the night.

Every inmate was responsible for cleaning her own pod, and incentives were provided for the person who did the best job. The person who had the cleanest room got to keep two videos for three days and could watch the movies on a TV cart in her pod.

The facility is equipped with doctors, nurses, an infirmary and a hospital triage area. Sally made several trips to the infirmary during her stay, first to get Betadine swabs to care for the stitches still in her foot from surgery. She also requested Metamucil to help with an ongoing colon problem. It took a while to be able to use her CPAP machine.

The jail was also equipped with a dentist for emergencies like pulling an abscessed tooth.

But still, jail was jail.

* * *

"I couldn't believe it was happening, that I was sitting in jail. But I probably handled it better than most; in some ways it was like camping out," she said.

She had just had surgery on her wrist and her right ankle, and there was a pin in her second toe to correct claw toe.

"I was wearing a surgical boot, which I had to wear for the entire time—sixty-one days—because my tennis shoes got wet and I had to throw them away. The first thing I did when I was released from jail was get rid of that surgical boot," she said with a slight laugh.

She had to make do with the jail-issue shampoo and soap, which was pretty harsh on her sensitive skin and colored hair.

"I didn't have any money to buy anything," Sally said Detective Henson told her, saying she wouldn't need any money when he arrested her.

At first the staff at the jail were routinely as unpleasant as possible.

Still nursing the remnants of surgery on her right foot, Sally would go to the infirmary for Betadine swabs and other medical needs. It wasn't pleasant.

"When I wanted some Metamucil for a colon problem—not for constipation—the nurse in the infirmary said, "I'm a nurse, too, Miss Hill, and Metamucil isn't used for that."

Sally said she tried to remain pleasant to everyone, and eventually the staff became a little more agreeable.

Sally's friends and church family from Good News Ministries were incredibly concerned about her physical and mental well-being when she was arrested. They rallied around her, trying to coordinate the thirty-minute visitation each week so everyone who wanted to visit her could, assuming she didn't need to meet with her defense team. They also kept prayer vigils going around the clock.

Patty Campbell said, "I feel so badly that she's been arrested and is in jail for a month. She must feel isolated and abandoned. Seeing those pictures of her in a red jumpsuit with her hands and feet shackled breaks my heart. I know Sally didn't do this. I would trust her with my life.

"I know she must think she is in a nightmare. I know if she could trade her life for that patient's, she would."

Friend Diane Thomas' concern for her friend was all too evident: "She was crushed and devastated. She was still living with the backlash of the chemicals she had in her from the chemotherapy.

"I feel so sorry for her, she must feel so alone. There is no way she did this. There just isn't any way . . . she doesn't have a mean bone in her body."

Clearly it made Sally feel better to get much-needed support from friends and church members while she was in jail. It also boosted her spirits when she began to hear from people who didn't know her, but had heard her story and wanted to encourage her.

"The first couple of days I was in jail, I got a couple of letters, and by the end of my stay, about three hundred and fifty people had communicated with me, telling me to keep the faith," she recalled with pride. "I had half of Charlotte praying for me."

But, for the most part, the days were long and hard, emotionally. She could get books from the library, she could write notes, play board games with other inmates and watch TV.

The only exposure she had to the outside was a courtyard—much like a brick room with a screened window, with no view of the outside, that had a basketball hoop at one end. Most of the women used the area just to get a breath of fresh air and walk around and talk to each other.

A day after her incarceration, Sally had a preliminary hearing. She and her attorney were summoned to the video suite to meet with the judge via teleconferencing. When asked if she understood the charges against her, Sally said she did. She would be notified when there would be a bond hearing.

A few weeks into her incarceration, Sally called her mother Alice, who was being cared for in a home because of her Alzheimer's.

"Where are you?" Alice asked, because she had been accustomed to talking to Sally and seeing her on a regular basis.

"Mama, remember, I'm in jail. . . . I told you about it." Immediately her mother began to cry.

Attorney John Golding, who'd represented Sally in the malpractice suit filed by Sandra Joyner's estate, was one of the first people to see Sally after her arrest.

"She was crushed and humiliated. 'Desolate' is the best way to describe it," he told a reporter.

At a September 25 bond hearing, more than a dozen church members were on hand to support her, along with people she had worked with.

Sandra's sister sat alone in the courtroom.

Sally was brought into the courtroom wearing a red jail uniform with her wrists and legs in shackles. It was clear she was having a hard time looking at her friends when she entered the room. She would look up and then away from her supporters before she could muster up a forced half-smile.

Beth Freeman, the assistant district attorney, had specifically asked that Sally not be released on bond. "She has stated that she would do nothing different in treating Sandra Joyner. And that is sad, considering that Sandra Joyner died," Freeman told the judge. "This definitely is the only person who gave Sandra Joyner medicine on this [sic] day, and Sandra Joyner is dead."

Sally's public defenders, Susan Weigand and Jean Lawson, pointed out that Sandra's death had been ruled a medical accident five years earlier. They specifically questioned why witnesses who supposedly heard Sally say that Sandra had stolen her boyfriend in high school hadn't given that information to civil attorneys when they were interviewed under oath years ago.

It was during that hearing that Detective Henson told the judge that Sally had given Sandra more of a potent painkiller than first believed, saying that it had been discovered after Sandra's death that an additional 5 ccs of fentanyl was missing and the prosecution believed that Sally had given it to Sandra in the recovery room. He also told the judge that Sally had admitted to altering a medication log that recorded the use of the drug.

However, defense attorneys challenged the new information, pointing out that it had not been discovered during investigations by the state medical and nursing boards and the civil lawyer in the medical malpractice suit filed by Sandra's husband, John Joyner, in 2003. Defense attorneys also reminded the judge that drug logs are changed all the time.

"There is no evidence that Miss Hill knowingly, deliberately selected this person and killed her," Jean Lawson said in court. "The suggestion that this is a product of a thirty-year grudge is outrageous."

Attorney John Golding was on hand to speak on Sally's behalf, saying he had studied the case at length after Sandra's death and he had continued to believe in Sally's innocence.

Sally's friends, and people who had worked with her previously, strongly disagreed with the prosecution, telling the judge that Sally was innocent of any crime and deserved to be released on bond.

"There was nothing I saw to suggest that she was likely

to hold a grudge for thirty years. She's not that kind of person, she's really nurturing and nice; she's serious and concerned.

"It seems to me at most you could say maybe this was misjudgment about the effects of fentanyl. . . ." Golding told the judge.

Later, speaking on Sally's behalf, John Golding told *People* magazine, "I have seen nothing that would indicate she was capable of murder.

"I would be really surprised to learn any different."

Sally's pastor Ron Jackson told the judge, "She's innocent. She's innocent of the crime, we're praying for her and I believe the Lord will deliver her."

But the prosecutors said they would prove that Sally Hill was a killer.

That day in court, Detective Henson revealed new information when he testified that Sally had given Sandra Joyner more medication than originally thought. It was initially believed that Sally had given Sandra 5 ccs of fentanyl in the operating room and another 2 ccs, one at a time, in the recovery room after Sandra complained of pain.

But Detective Henson said it was later discovered that an additional 5 ccs of the painkiller were missing from the doctor's office after Sandra's death, 5 ccs the prosecution believed Sally had given Sandra in addition to the 7 ccs she had documented on the medication log.

He also said that in the nursing board investigation, Sally had admitted to turning off the audible alarm that would have sounded when Sandra went into respiratory arrest and offered no explanation.

When it became apparent that Sandra was in trouble, two co-workers had asked Sally if her patient was OK, he recounted.

"She told them Sandra was fine. This was while she was sitting at a desk eating a biscuit.

"The defendant, according to all of the witnesses, rendered no assistance in life-saving procedures," he said later.

In 2003 the medical board charged that Sally had acted largely on her own, and when Sandra went into respiratory distress, Sally "repeatedly declined offers of assistance from other staff members and directed them not to summon Dr. Tucker."

Susan Weigand, assistant public defender on Sally's case, told the judge that throughout the civil case—which had been settled in 2003—and a thorough medical investigation, nobody had even suggested that a crime had been committed. She said that Dr. Tucker, who was later disciplined by the medical board for not properly supervising Sally, had previously said he would trust Sally to put him—even his children—to sleep for surgery.

In the end, Jean Lawson referred to the state's case as "pretty speculative."

Several medical professionals were in the courtroom to tell the judge about their relationships with Sally, whom they called "caring," "loving," "professional" and "innocent."

Sally tried to acknowledge them occasionally with a feeble smile, but she never stood or spoke during the hearing. On occasion she would bite her lip, and sometimes cried.

In contrast to what most anesthetists outside the Charlotte area say, Dr. Lee Ann McGinnis of Charlotte's Presbyterian Hospital, one of three anesthesiologists who spoke on Sally's behalf, presented a very different view, saying that fentanyl is often used in office-based surgery because it works fast and is metabolized quickly. However, it was unclear whether she was referring to the use of fentanyl during surgery or in the recovery room.

She also said that the dose given would depend on the length of the surgery and the patient's metabolism.

Two ccs of fentanyl administered in the recovery room "is not a significant amount," McGinnis told the judge, according to a newspaper report, which is in contrast to other people who are familiar with fentanyl.

"Today thousands and thousands of people are going to have that dose of fentanyl."

Dr. Mark Romanoff, president of the Mecklenburg County Medical Society, said that fentanyl is used millions of times a week, though he didn't specify whether he was referring to its use during surgery or afterward as a pain medication.

"You don't have to be scared that you've received fentanyl. It's an excellent medication [and] has a great safety profile," he explained.

At the hearing Detective Henson told the judge that fentanyl was "one hundred times more powerful than morphine." It was Detective Henson's theory that Sally had given Sandra an additional 5 ccs, which was unaccounted for that day, instead of the 2 ccs that Sally had reported.

Henson went on to quote an emergency room doctor who said that 7 ccs of fentanyl in the recovery room "would have been lethal," adding that Percocet was generally used for pain after surgery.

But McGinnis didn't agree that 7 ccs would be too much. "People sometimes get that much."

McGinnis confirmed that fentanyl is more potent than morphine, she guessed probably eighty times more powerful. But she said the difference is adjusted for in the dosage.

"Eight milligrams of fentanyl would be eighty times as

potent as eight milligrams of morphine, but she never got eight milligrams of fentanyl," McGinnis explained.

Whether 12 ccs of fentanyl would have been dangerous for Sandra "depends on a lot of things," Karen Lucisano, director of the nurse anesthesia program at Carolinas Medical Center, said. "It depends on the length of the operation and when the last dosage was given. If you drink or smoke, or take other kinds of painkillers on a regular basis, you can need massive doses," she said.

Lucisano emphasized her position by saying, "I've had patients that I've given twelve ccs in the IV [in the operating room] and they were still talking."

Dr. Romanoff summed it up by saying, "It's not black or white. It's a very gray area in terms of guidelines and how much medication you use."

The prosecution told the judge that Sally had admitted turning off the alarm on the device that was monitoring Sandra's breathing, which would have alerted the other nurses that Sandra was in trouble, but why it was turned off is still a mystery, because so far Sally has not discussed any of the charges against her, nor has she made an official plea of guilty or not guilty.

McGinnis told the judge that surgeons sometimes ask to have the alarm turned off when they are performing certain procedures. But normally, in the hospital, she said, the alarm is on throughout the surgery and recovery period.

However, according to Dr. Romanoff, "Just turning off the alarm itself is not necessarily a red flag if there was an appropriate reason to do that."

He also said that it is not unusual to get false positives with the alarm.

"Sometimes, if the patient is shivering, you will get a lot of false alarms or if the patient is cold, there may be some reason to temporarily turn off the alarm so that you don't get a lot of false alarms."

Regardless, Sandra's death was tragic, said McGinnis, who had worked with Sally, and whose son went to school with one of Sandra's sons.

"I don't want to add to this tragedy by having somebody else's life ruined," she told those in the hearing.

At the end of the day, District Court Judge Phil Howerton declined to set bond for Sally, although he said she probably deserved it. It was his policy to let a Superior Court judge make that decision in murder cases.

That hearing didn't take place until November 9, 2006.

At the second bond hearing, Sally's court-appointed attorneys argued that Sandra's death was not intentional and said that if it had been, it would have been discovered a long time ago.

"I think what happened that day was a tragic accident," Susan Weigand said.

Sally's lawyers told the judge that she had suffered a bout of leukemia after Sandra's death, and didn't fight the suspension by the North Carolina Board of Nursing because she was too sick to work.

John Golding, who felt the need to stand up for Sally, told the judge that she should be allowed to leave jail without bond, which prompted several of her friends to say "Amen" under their breath.

Assistant District Attorney Beth Freeman told the judge that Sally had turned off an alarm that would have alerted co-workers to the fact that Sandra was having trouble breathing. She also said Sally had given Sandra more fentanyl than was first believed and admitted altering a log that recorded use of the drug.

It was also brought up that witnesses had reported hearing Sally say in 1999 that Sandra had stolen her high school boyfriend.

"She has stated that she would do nothing different in treating Sandra Joyner. And that is sad, considering Sandra Joyner died," Beth Freeman told the judge.

The courtroom was nearly full for the hearing, with the front rows filled with members of Sally's church and her co-workers.

Sally's defense attorneys asked for the bond to be set at $50,000; however, Judge Albert Diaz decided that she could be released on a $100,000 secured bond, and bailiffs led her from the court.

Sally saw the $100,000 bond as a sign from heaven.

"I believe that was a prayer answered. They don't usually let someone get out of jail on a murder charge, but the judge said they didn't have enough evidence to hold me. No one leaves jail on a first-degree murder charge with a hundred thousand dollars bond—that was God's divine intervention."

That night, around 7 p.m., Sally was finally free to leave the Mecklenburg County Jail. Her close friend Ronda Jackson, Reverend Ron Jackson's wife, brought some tennis shoes for Sally to wear home; she could finally throw away the surgical boot that she had been wearing for over two months.

Ronda Jackson told a local reporter that their only stop on the way home would be at the store for Sally to get some coffee creamer, saying "she really likes good coffee."

Then they headed home to Weddington. At last Sally would see her four cats, who were like children to her. She had been worried about them the whole time she was in jail, concerned because they weren't used to being alone for such long periods of time.

Of course, friends had been good about feeding and caring for them, but that's not the same as a "mother's"

TLC and the attention they get when she is at home with them.

On that damp and cold night, bundled up in a yellow rain slicker, carrying a half-empty bottle of Sun-Drop soda, Sally left the jail and filed past the throng of reporters who had gathered in the underground parking area of the jail where she would be processed any minute.

The reporters pushed and shoved to get closer to Sally, all jockeying for a better position.

"Did you mean to kill Sandra Joyner?" one reporter yelled to Sally as the television camera lights panned in on her.

Her response was a diabolical-sounding laugh that was shocking and difficult to watch later on the 11 p.m. news that night and the next day. It would not play well at trial.

TWENTY-SEVEN

Detective Henson

Detective Chuck Henson had been with the Charlotte-Mecklenburg Police Department for fourteen years, and was promoted to the position of detective in November 2000.

He was the lead Homicide cold case detective in the department, the only one working the Sandra Joyner investigation full time, although he did have the help of a couple of assistants. After the case was turned over to the prosecutor in September 2007, Detective Henson was promoted to sergeant and given responsibility for training and supervising twenty-one officers on the second shift.

However, when Sally's trial does begin, he will be in court, serving as the lead detective on the case again, since he is the one who investigated it.

Dr. Tucker has said that he told the medical board investigators in 2003 of his suspicions about Sally's intent, saying, "I think there is an element of malicious behavior here," but the police department did not investigate his suspicions until four years later.

In January 2007 when District Attorney Peter Gilchrist was anonymously presented with new information, it was decided to reopen the case of Sandra Joyner's death. Beth

Freeman, assistant district attorney, approached the Homicide Cold Case unit's Captain Sean Mulhall, Detective Henson's supervisor, asking him to check out the information to determine if they should reopen the case as a homicide.

Charlotte-Mecklenburg Police Captain Mulhall, who oversees homicide investigations, has said that police didn't investigate right away because medical examiners had ruled Sandra's death an accident, and nobody alleged any wrongdoing. Apparently the North Carolina Medical Board had not passed along Dr. Tucker's comments about Sally's suspected motive. With this new information at hand, Captain Mulhall gave the assignment to Detective Henson, asking him to look into Sandra's death to see if there was any validity to the new allegations.

"He asked me to see what I thought," said Detective Henson, who was in his late thirties then, 5'10" with a shaven head and piercing blue eyes. His clean-cut looks are deceiving; the father of a toddler and a new baby looks much younger than he actually is. In fact, his boyish appearance makes it difficult to imagine the vast experience he already has.

But he had a formidable record as a plainclothes detective. Years earlier his persistence led to the apprehension of a sought-after serial killer when Detective Henson's quick thinking led him to get DNA off a cigarette butt the perpetrator casually dropped on the street.

Since April 2001, Detective Henson has handled as many as seventy cases, at least half of which have been cleared. In fact he cleared more than any other detective in the department, including his first cold case, which was twenty-one years old when he reopened it.

The Sally Hill case wasn't his first high-profile cold case either; he had several others: A man who kidnapped a Charlotte teen in 1964 was sentenced to death row; a

double murderer has been confined to a Virginia prison
for life; he also solved a forty-five-year-old case.

Covering cold cases is an especially difficult job. Trails
go dry, evidence becomes degraded. But in some ways time
gives cold case detectives an advantage. Alibis become en-
emies. Ex-wives and ex-partners, once too loyal to talk,
give investigators an earful. Fearful witnesses sometimes
feel that time has made them safe from retribution.

Cold case work is about persistence, being close to the
street, knowing how to scare up folks who might be a little more inclined to speak now that some time has passed.
These people often feel they have a special sense of duty
to speak for the victims.

Like so many of his high-profile cases, Sally Hill's story
took on a life of its own when *The Charlotte Observer* and
the Raleigh *News & Observer* began running stories every
day, along with local and statewide television stations.

It didn't take long for the story to be propelled into the
national and international spotlight with *People* magazine, *USA Today*, *Inside Edition*, MSNBC and *Nancy
Grace* joining the fray and savoring every detail. Even after the other media outlets stopped running the story, *48
Hours* had begun work on a segment scheduled to air right
before Sally Hill goes to trial.

After reading the file on Sandra Joyner's death in
2001, which consisted of massive amounts of malpractice
paperwork, nursing and medical board hearings and other
findings, Detective Henson began talking to the people
who knew Sandra and Sally best, from high school up to
the time of Sandra's death.

Initially he thought it was going to be a routine case, one
that might not even turn up anything that would be considered a crime. After all, Sandra's death had been ruled a
horrible accident five years earlier. It would be a long way
to go to accuse someone of murder at this late date.

But the more Detective Henson talked to people who knew the women, especially those who went to high school with them, the more he felt he needed to dig deeper into the history of the two classmates.

"At first I thought, 'No one could hold a grudge for that long,'" he said. But the more he talked to people, the more he began to think there might be something there.

Then in May, Detective Henson and his partner showed up at Sally's front door, unannounced. They rang the doorbell and stood there stoically waiting for her to appear.

Unsuspecting, Sally was cordial and invited them into the house. Detective Henson explained that he was investigating Sandra Joyner's death, that the case had been reopened. Sally willingly spoke with the detectives for over an hour and a half.

However, while answering their questions, she apparently displayed what some considered a cavalier attitude during the nursing board investigation in 2003, when she'd made inappropriate comments like "Only me and Sandra and Jesus know what happened in that room."

In his gut, Detective Henson had begun to feel that there was more to the story than he first thought. In fact, it was then that he began to feel as if Sally probably was guilty of killing Sandra, intentionally and with forethought.

Detective Henson tried several times to talk to Sally again, but after their initial meeting, she had lawyered up; John Golding, her attorney in the 2003 malpractice suit, had advised her not to talk to the police anymore. Detective Henson was also never able to talk to Sally's estranged husband, Jim, or anyone else in the Hill family.

Nine months later, when Detective Henson had finished meeting with everyone who knew the parties involved, he presented his findings to Marcia Goodman of the Homicide Unit. Coincidentally, all of the Homicide district attorneys were meeting in Charlotte that week, so she asked Detective Henson to share his findings with the entire group to get their feel for the case.

Within hours, the district attorney issued an arrest warrant for Sally Hill, saying that there was probable cause to believe that she did "unlawfully, wilfully and feloniously and of malice aforethought kill and murder Sandra Baker Joyner."

"Cold cases are different from homicides; they are held to a higher standard," a detective explained. "You have to show probable cause. The case is then reviewed, and you have to have the district attorney's approval before you can arrest a suspect."

It was not until September 8, 2006, that Detective Henson would see Sally Hill again.

Once again unannounced, the detective and his partner drove into the quiet Weddington neighborhood where the houses were far enough apart that neighbors had no idea what was going on unless they were deliberately watching.

The detective pulled up in Sally's driveway and parked the unmarked vehicle.

He pressed the doorbell and waited for Sally to come to the front door. She seemed puzzled at the sight of Detective Henson, and said she couldn't talk on advice of her attorney. She said he told her they would have to arrest her and called a female officer to stay with her while she dressed.

"I was in shock. I had on my housecoat getting ready to take a shower," she explained.

She was allowed to call her mother and let her know she wasn't coming for lunch, cancel a chiropractic appointment, and call a neighbor to feed the cats for a couple of days. The neighbor called a cat sitter Sally had used before. After 61 days in jail Sally had a hefty cat-sitting bill. Sally was solemn as he helped her into the backseat of the car for the twenty-five-minute drive uptown to the Mecklenburg County Jail.

Sally was limping and wearing what Detective Henson thought was a plastic bandage on her right foot. However, friends explained that she had just had surgery and was wearing a surgical boot.

Sally was quiet during the ride to the jail, where she was booked and fingerprinted before being issued the standard red jumpsuit.

While being processed, she was told that her long platinum-colored hair, which had been held back with a large clip, had to be undone. After she removed the large barrette, Sally ran her fingers through her hair and it fell to her shoulders. Her permanent black eyeliner, in contrast to her very fair complexion and light hair, made for a garish mug shot.

Sally Jordan Hill would stand trial for the first-degree murder of her one-time patient and former high school classmate Sandra Joyner. Although she would not face the death penalty, she would be looking at spending the rest of her life in prison if she was found guilty.

TWENTY-EIGHT

Tucker: Hill Out of Control

It was not until October 2003 that Dr. Tucker's comment about Sally Hill being out of control on the day of Sandra's death came to light. At the time his deposition was taken, it could not be made public, but when the medical board changed their ruling, the deposition was given to *The Charlotte Observer* and *USA Today*. It was also the first time that the public learned that Sandra had been connected to an EKG monitor instead of a pulse oximeter, which police thought could be a critical discovery.

The police department's murder charge against Sally was based in large part on the information provided in Dr. Tucker's deposition—her comment in 1999 about Sandra stealing her high school boyfriend, the report of additional fentanyl that was missing and the fact that the drug log had been changed.

All that, coupled with the fact that Sally had appeared to have done nothing to help Sandra when she was in respiratory arrest, seemed to be the basis for the prosecution's case.

District Attorney Peter Gilchrist declined to say when his office had been contacted with allegations of foul play in Sandra's death. He would only say that it would be inappropriate for him to talk about the case while charges were still pending.

However, Charlotte-Mecklenburg police Captain Sean Mulhall, who oversees homicide investigations, said the police department didn't investigate immediately after Sandra's death because the medical examiner had ruled the death an accident, and at the time no one had alleged any wrongdoing.

The police maintained that prosecutors got an anonymous tip early in 2007, with new information, and asked the police department to look into the matter to see if there was anything to the new allegations.

The Charlotte Observer reported that North Carolina Medical Board lawyer Thomas Mansfield said Dr. Tucker's allegations that Sally had committed a crime had not been turned over to police because state law at the time prohibited the medical board from sharing information with law enforcement agencies. Legislators have since changed the law.

Neither Dr. Tucker nor Sally ever told the medical board that there was any animosity between Sally and Sandra; however Dr. Tucker did say during the medical board investigation that he knew the women had a "prior relationship" and he wondered whether that might have led to Sally's behavior the day that Sandra died.

"I don't know if [Sandra] said something that was the straw that broke the camel's back. I don't know what happened," Dr. Tucker said at the time of his deposition.

Sally never denied that she'd known Sandra casually in school. She told the medical board that Sandra had been a grade ahead of her and had been a judge when Sally had tried out for cheerleader at Smith Junior High School in the late 1960s.

The two girls had mutual friends, but didn't socialize together, Sally explained.

"I don't ever remember going to her house. I would see her and her then-boyfriend [John] walk around school together because he was in football and she was a cheerleader or letter girl, something like that."

Sally also told the board that she and Sandra had talked about their high school days in 1999, when Sandra had come to Dr. Tucker's office for her first surgery.

"She was in the process of going through a divorce," Sally said referring to a conversation that actually took place in 2001, not 1999, as she'd told investigators.

"She kept going on about her life and how tragic it had been in the past year."

The prosecutor alleged that Sally had turned off the alarm that would have alerted co-workers to Sandra's breathing problems. In his deposition, Dr. Tucker recalled something he considered odd about the scenario—Sandra had been connected to an EKG, which he felt was highly unusual. (Other nurse anesthetists have said it is not unusual to have a patient connected to an EKG in recovery.) However, Sandra should have been connected to a pulse oximeter, which monitors breathing and was supposed to make a regular beeping sound that changes in tone as a patient's breathing varies, as Dr. Tucker explained. Detective Henson said publicly that Sally admitted turning off the alarm.

From his office next to the recovery room, Dr. Tucker said he could hear a monitor beeping, and that from the tone, he believed Sandra was breathing normally.

Dr. Tucker maintained that the EKG monitor made a similar sound to a pulse oximeter, but it didn't detect changes in breathing. Later, he said he realized he might have been hearing the EKG instead of the pulse oximeter, but that raises the question "Would the EKG monitor also signal an alarm indicating that Sandra was in trouble?" It would signal an alarm, but it would indicate heart failure rather than respiratory difficulties.

None of Sally's co-workers noticed whether the pulse oximeter was turned off, Tucker said.

During the 2003 investigation, Sally told the nursing board that shortly after the second dose of fentanyl she "noticed the pulse ox was off. The first thing I noticed was the pulse ox had dropped. I went and got Robinul and ephedrine. I keep it drawn up," she told the investigator.

Mecklenburg County prosecutors have said that they believe that the additional 5 ccs of fentanyl that was missing from the office—supposedly signed out by Sally for the next surgery in the afternoon on April 10, before Sandra's death—were instead given to Sandra in the recovery room. That means Sandra could have been given 5 ccs of fentanyl in surgery and another 7 ccs, instead of 2, in the recovery room, which could have been deadly.

Sally has adamantly denied giving Sandra more than 7 ccs. She told the medical board that she signed out another 5 ccs for a second patient who was to have surgery that afternoon, but that she discarded it when the surgery was canceled after Sandra's death.

Dr. Tucker testified that it was odd for Sally to sign out two doses of fentanyl—5 ccs for the next patient and 2 ccs for Joyner—when she could have given Sandra what she already had on hand, since she had signed out 5 ccs for the next patient.

Dr. Tucker testified that he had asked Sally why she'd written in the drug log that she had withdrawn 5 ccs on April 11 (instead of April 10) when all the cases had been canceled after Sandra's death.

"The only reason somebody would change that date," Tucker said, "is, they started thinking about it, and they were feeling guilty because they had done something wrong."

But when the investigator questioned Sally about the discrepancy, she testified that she didn't know why she had marked out the 10th and written in the 11th.

"I was a little upset at that point. This was when we were finishing the day up after the incident," she said, referring to Sandra's death.

Could she have given Sandra a total of 12 ccs of fentanyl? the investigator asked.

"No way," Sally said emphatically. "She had seven ccs, and that's what's documented right here," she told the investigator, pointing to the medication log.

When the medical examiner conducted the autopsy on Sandra's body in 2001, he might have been able to tell exactly how much fentanyl was in Sandra's system; however, if her body were exhumed now, it would not be possible, medical experts say.

The issue of how much fentanyl was in Sandra's body at the time of her death would seem to be relatively easy to answer. However, when contacted, the Mecklenburg County Medical Examiner's Office was irate that the question would even be asked.

"We're not in the business of answering these kind of questions, that's not our job," said the person who answered the phone, possibly one of the medical examiners. "You can hire a toxicologist to answer that question," he scoffed.

He also declined to clarify any information in the autopsy about other drugs found in Sandra's body, those she was thought to have been taking for anxiety or depression.

As mentioned before, another point of contention between Dr. Tucker and Sally was whether she had the authority to administer fentanyl for patients in the recovery room at all.

Sally said she had done it "millions of times," and that Dr. Tucker had never told her to stop.

"I mean, if someone has huge lips and they can't swallow and they're screaming and crying in pain, I just didn't see any reason not to give her fentanyl," she said.

But Dr. Tucker insisted: "I never knew she was doing it."

TWENTY-NINE

Due Process

As the months dragged on, everyone forgot about Sally Hill. The summer came and went. Durham's District Attorney Mike Nifong made headlines by tarnishing the reputations of three Duke lacrosse players when, as it turned out, he had never had any real evidence that an exotic dancer had been raped and beaten by the boys, as she had claimed.

Some speculate that the Hill case might be dropped, considering the headlines seen around the world in the spring about the antics of Durham District Attorney Mike Nifong, who claimed to have a solid case against three Duke lacrosse players. A year after he accused the students of raping a dancer at an off-campus party, it was discovered, primarily because of the intense digging of eleven defense attorneys representing the boys, that Nifong had absolutely no proof of any of the allegations and had, in fact, covered up evidence to the contrary.

His egregious acts against the innocent young men led to his being disbarred and kicked out of office. The over-zealous district attorney, whose sole intention seemed to be getting elected in November 2007, was an embarrassment to the North Carolina judicial system as a whole. And some now think highly visible cases might surely make district attorneys take a second look before taking a weak case to court.

North Carolina had been humiliated by the unthinkable miscarriage of justice purported by Nifong, and some wondered if the Charlotte district attorney was having second thoughts about taking Sally Hill to trial.

Sergeant Henson immediately put that theory to rest.

"This district attorney does just the opposite [as Nifong did]. She is diligent about making sure she has the evidence necessary to take someone to trial," he explained, referring to assistant District Attorney Beth Freeman, who is handling the case.

The delays, month after month, were due to the administrative process, which would take the case forward to an arraignment and then finally a trial date, he said. That, he believed, probably wouldn't happen until the summer of 2008, in spite of the fact that documents at the courthouse indicate that the trial had been scheduled for March.

Still, Detective Henson remains convinced that he knows what Sally and the defense team will do.

"I fully expect her to plead not guilty," he said emphatically. "And what the public knows about the case at this point is just the tip of the iceberg," he said mysteriously.

Back at the Weddington house that Sally so loved, instead of decorating for Christmas, she was getting it fixed up so she could put it on the market and sell it.

A small hand-made "For Sale" sign sat near the driveway entrance. It did not have the name of a realtor on it, merely a phone number to call if anyone was interested in seeing the house, which property records indicate was in Sally's name, alone. The house, which was purchased for $78,000 in 1983, is now estimated to be worth almost three times that.

Sally's mother Alice is living in a nursing home where

she can be cared for around the clock—the same home where Sally's father LeGette lived until his death in January 2006.

Sally visits her mother often and takes her to her doctors' appointments, although she admits her mother can get cantankerous on occasion.

"Sometimes she gets sassy with me. She wears the same clothes every day and she gets mad when I mention it," Sally said, sounding more like the mother than the daughter.

"So now I say, 'Mama, you would say something to me if I wore the same clothes every day, wouldn't you?'"

That seems to register with her mother, whose Alzheimer's was diagnosed early enough that she could begin taking medication to slow the process. She is not sure her mother understands the gravity of her situation, what it means for her daughter to be on trial for first-degree murder.

"When I called her and told her I was in jail, she cried," said Sally.

But the next time Sally mentioned the case, it was as if her mother was hearing it for the first time.

Sally explained that she had been able to make sure her father, who'd had a number of health problems, and her mother were in a good home with around-the-clock care, because her mother's sister had paid for it.

"I was always close to my mother, but when I came back to the Lord, I was able to forgive my father then." She says she and her father were always at odds, fighting about everything. "We were too much alike." But in the months before his death they made their peace.

"My mother only went to the eighth grade. She worked at Lance [the cracker and cookie company] before I was born, then quit work to stay home with me," Sally explained. When Sally was in high school, her mother was the resident manager of the apartments where they lived until she retired.

Sally is afraid she won't be able to keep her mother in the home much longer after the money her aunt earmarked for her sister's care runs out.

Sally has lost everything—her career, her health, her marriage and any money she might have had saved for the future.

"Sally has had it tough . . . life has kicked her in the ass—but that doesn't mean she killed someone," cautioned Ronnie Stack.

Court-appointed defense attorneys are representing Sally on the murder charge, because she was not able to afford a private defense attorney, something other nurses find unbelievable, since nurse anesthetists make such good money.

"I've cut back on everything. I only have the garbage picked up once a week now, I've cut the television cable back to just the basics," she added.

Now her life revolves around her cats, who are like her children.

When Jim moved out two years earlier, Sally had her 13-year-old white cat, Oscar, who she loved like an old friend. But sadly, since then, she has had to put Oscar to sleep.

Then, when Jim moved out, he left Winston, who was actually his cat, for Sally to care for. Jim didn't want to take Winston, a senior in cat years, to live in an apartment with him.

"Jim didn't want to pay a five-hundred-dollar pet deposit when he rented the apartment. He was concerned because Winston sprays [which is how males mark their territory]. I told him the cat probably wouldn't spray if he was there by himself, if Winston was the only cat and Jim paid a lot of attention to him, he wouldn't try to mark his territory," she explained. Still Jim left Winston with her.

Since then she has had to put Winston down. "Jim doesn't even know," she said sadly. Last year when Sally was introduced to Sarah, a tortoiseshell cat, she could not resist bringing her home to "join the family." Her latest adoption was her cat George.

Sally had a couple of teenage girls helping her care for the house and packing up all of her belongings, but some days the depression is too great, sometimes it is all she can do to put one foot in front of the other to accomplish the basics—to keep the litter box from smelling and the cat food from being strewn around the house, for instance.

If she can rally for anything, though, it is to see that her mother keeps her doctors' appointments and that the cats are well cared for.

"I was worried to death about them while I was in jail. People would go over and feed them, but they weren't used to spending so much time alone," she explained.

Right after her arrest, Sally's mother-in-law Anita Hill told a *People* magazine reporter that Jim, her son and Sally's estranged husband, was really upset about what Sally was going through.

"He's taking this very hard. We're all concerned," she said.

Yet Jim has refused to talk to any of the media on his wife's behalf, even to clear up misconceptions about whether she could hold a grudge for thirty years.

In fact, many of the people who initially talked to reporters when Sandra's death and the investigation into Sally's involvement became public will not talk to anyone now, including those closest to her—friends and family, church members and Sally's former lawyer.

Shortly before Sandra's death, Jim had to quit his job with UPS because of knee problems. Not too long afterwards, he decided to go back to school to become a teacher. He moved out of the Weddington house in 2005.

Sally says the couple have filed for divorce, but they are still hammering out a property settlement.

According to Sally, at first Jim didn't want anything, but as time has gone by, they have begun squabbling over everything. Sally senses that he has moved on to another life and wants her and her troubles behind him.

"I wish he would speak up for me," Sally said, lowering her voice, "but he's in the process of becoming a teacher. Maybe he thinks it wouldn't be good for his new career."

When she and Jim separated over two years ago, she put away all the wedding pictures and other mementos of happier and more promising times in her life. Now she is sorting through all her belongings, unpacking her wedding dress, which has been sealed away for twenty-five years, hoping she can sell it.

"My mother always told me to keep it, in case I had a daughter. But it probably wouldn't have worked out. My mother was 5'2", one hundred and two pounds—and when I got married I was 5' 8", one hundred and thirty-five pounds, so her dress wouldn't fit me."

Sorting through her keepsakes and treasures has opened a Pandora's box of memories, some happy, far too many sad.

Sally had worked hard to become a registered nurse and ultimately a nurse anesthetist. She didn't let finances stop her from fulfilling her dream; she found a way to put herself through school and to excel in her class.

She had established a lucrative and rewarding career, but never fulfilled her dreams of moving from Charlotte to New York, where she could spread her wings, or of having a family.

Eventually Sally had returned to her religious foundation, which Jim resisted becoming involved in; her parents were ill and needed round-the-clock care for their health problems, and Jim wouldn't help with them, either, in spite of Sally's leukemia diagnosis. The rest is history.

In spite of all that has happened, only two things remain constant in Sally's life—her faith in God, and her belief that she will be found innocent of the charges that have been brought against her.

"I don't know, maybe God has something in store for me. Maybe I will end up being able to educate nurses about what can happen to them in the nursing field, like it did me."

Sounding wistful, she added, "I know there's a reason for all this! I know God has a plan!"

THIRTY

Time Drags On

In September 2007, Detective Henson told local Judge Phil Howerton at a bond hearing that Sally Hill had turned off an alarm that would have alerted co-workers to the fact that Sandra was having trouble breathing.

He also said that it had been discovered that an additional 5 ccs of fentanyl had been missing on the day of Sandra's death, and he believed Sally had given Sandra more than first believed. He pointed out that Sally had admitted to altering a log that day that recorded use of the drug.

Sally's lawyers countered the charges by telling the judge that Sandra had died from a medical accident, as it had been ruled more than five years before. They questioned why witnesses who supposedly heard Hill say Sandra stole her boyfriend in high school didn't give that information to civil attorneys when they were originally interviewed under oath.

They also asked why the supposedly missing drugs weren't discovered during investigations by the state medical board, state nursing board and civil lawyers in a medical malpractice suit filed by John Joyner on behalf of Sandra's estate.

"There is no evidence that Miss Hill knowingly, deliberately selected this person and killed her," Public Defender Jean Lawson said in court. "The suggestion that this is a product of a thirty-year grudge is outrageous."

Detective Henson said that witnesses had heard Sally make the "boyfriend" comment when Sandra was at the Center for Cosmetic and Plastic Surgery for a first procedure in 1999, when Sally had put Sandra to sleep for her surgery.

Detective Henson also told the judge that Sally said she gave Sandra five cubic centimeters of fentanyl in the operating room and another two ccs, one at a time, in the recovery room after she complained of pain.

But Henson told the judge that five more ccs of the painkiller were missing from the doctor's office and he believed Hill gave it to Sandra.

Dr. Tucker has said that Sally didn't need to take another 5 ccs of fentanyl for the surgery that was supposed to be done in the afternoon, before Sandra's death. He implied that Sally had kept the drug in order to administer a larger dose to Sandra.

However, John O'Donnell, CRNA and Director of the Nurse Anesthesia Program at the University of Pittsburgh, takes issue with that theory.

"The nurse anesthetist usually puts the amount she is going to use for the individual surgery in a vial by itself. She doesn't combine the medication in one vial, there is a separate one for each patient," he explained.

"They just waste whatever is left over," he said explaining that when narcotics are wasted, another person is supposed to be present or it is captured on camera.

Or could the painkiller have been taken for another purpose, as some have speculated? Doctors and nurses have a fairly substantial incidence of becoming addicted to painkillers because of their ready availability.

The autopsy performed on Sandra showed that she had

died of drug poisoning, likely caused by fentanyl, but it is not clear how much was actually in her body.

Federal law requires nurses and doctors to account for every cubic centimeter of narcotics administered. Nurses commonly sign for drugs and keep a daily handwritten log of how much they use for each patient. The log is then returned to the pharmacy at the end of the day.

Detective Henson has said that Sally admitted to turning off an audible alarm, which would have sounded when Sandra went into respiratory arrest.

Detective Henson told the judge that when two co-workers asked Hill if her patient was OK, she told them that Sandra was fine.

"This was while she was sitting at a desk eating a biscuit," Detective Henson added.

Susan Weigand, Hill's other public defender, told the judge that throughout the civil case—which was settled in 2003—and a thorough medical investigation, nobody even suggested that a crime had been committed.

She said Dr. Tucker, later disciplined by the medical board for not properly supervising Sally, had earlier said that he would trust her to put him—even his children—to sleep. Jean Lawson went on to call the state's case "pretty speculative."

According to Dr. Tucker's Raleigh attorney Alan Schneider, the murder charge "is a significant development in the case," and was information that the board did not have before.

"Premeditated murder and gross negligence are two entirely different things," Schneider told a reporter.

When asked if Dr. Tucker will seek to have his record wiped clean, Schneider said he and his client have discussed how to proceed, but he would not comment further.

Sally's supporters—church members, medical professionals and her lawyer in the civil malpractice suit—filled nearly three rows in the courtroom. At the bond hearing, many of them talked to the judge about their relationship with Hill, calling her caring, loving, professional and innocent.

Several medical doctors and nurse anesthetists attested to Sally's character.

At the heart of the debate about fentanyl seems to be the distinction between fentanyl given during surgery and after surgery. No one seems to dispute the effectiveness of fentanyl in the IV during surgery, but it appears to be questionable as a pain medication after surgery unless it is given in minute doses.

Dr. Barry Friedberg, world-renowned anesthetist says, "The people who have testified to five ccs [250 micrograms] of fentanyl being given 'all the time' are in error if they believe this is a safe practice. It is not. Roughly that would be the equivalent of two hundred and fifty milligrams of Demerol!"

O'Donnell, who has headed up the nurse anesthesia program at the University of Pittsburgh since 1995 says, "Fentanyl is the common choice of drug for sedation because it is fast acting and it is common to give five to ten ccs during surgery."

However, morphine is the first choice for pain medication post-surgery, "except when the patient is in tremendous pain and needs relief quickly.

"Fentanyl is fairly robust and if given should only be administered one-half cc at a time post-operatively," he explained. "The nurse anesthetist should monitor the patient during surgery to see if there is any reaction to the fentanyl. If there are no problems during surgery (over a four-hour period), it can be administered in one-half cc increments after surgery.

"I've even given one cc post-operatively on occasion if the patient is in a great deal of pain; that's not unusual in Pennsylvania," he added.

Police also alleged that Sally had turned off the alarm on the device that was monitoring Sandra's breathing, a device called a pulse oximeter, that fits on a patient's index finger and records how much oxygen is in the blood.

With each heartbeat, a number appears on a monitor and the tone of the beep changes as the oxygen level decreases. When it reaches a certain level, the alarm goes off.

Karen Lucisano, who ran the Carolinas Medical Center nursing program, told the judge that some nurses turn off the alarm if they're facing the monitor because they can see the number and hear the change in tone, which would indicate a problem, long before they would hear an alarm.

"I don't even have to look at [it]," she said. "You can hear the change in the quality of the sound. Waiting for an alarm is a way late thing. We pick up changes long before that."

O'Donnell and other practicing CRNAs reinforce the importance of the patient being monitored at all times, especially using a pulse oximeter to make sure difficulties don't arise.

However, Lee Ann McGinnis said surgeons sometimes ask to have the alarm turned off while doing certain procedures, although she didn't say which ones. But normally, in the hospital, she said, the alarm is on throughout the entire period.

"Her death is tragic," said McGinnis, who had worked with Hill and whose son went to school with one of Sandra Joyner's sons. "I don't want to add to the tragedy by having somebody else's life ruined," she told the judge.

Month after month Sally has appeared in the appointed

courtroom at the Mecklenburg County Courthouse in up-town Charlotte for an administrative hearing. And every time, her case has been continued until the next month.

Defense attorney Susan Weigand has said she doesn't have all the disclosure she needs from the police depart-ment. Others say it is just the slow legal process. However, first-degree murder cases in nearby counties have come and gone in the time that Sally Hill has been awaiting her trial, including the high-profile case of Lisa Greene, a Cabarrus County mother found guilty of deliberately setting a fire in a mobile home, killing her two children in January 2006. By the end of 2007 she had been tried, found guilty and sen-tenced to life in prison.

Winter passes. Sally no longer has platinum blonde hair and the garish look of her mug shot created by per-manent eyeliner. As she sits in the middle row of the courtroom waiting for her case number to be called, no one seems to recognize her.

She is wearing glasses, her long hair, grayish with blonde streaks—more than likely her natural color. She is wearing a heavy wool sweater and skirt with opaque stock-ings. She has brought along a paperback book to pass the time and dull her senses.

Spring comes and goes, but still no word on when her trial will take place or why it is taking so long.

Detective Henson has said emphatically that the Char-lotte–Mecklenburg courts operate very differently than other jurisdictions. While he was not referring to the courts moving slowly, that certainly seems to be the case, as Sally doesn't even have a trial date yet.

While the legal wheels are turning, the medical com-munity is watching the case closely.

Since 2001, when Sandra Joyner died and information about the questionable circumstances of her death began to surface, the case has sparked a number of debates in the community. For example, is it wise for plastic surgeons to perform surgeries in their offices, which do not have the depth of emergency medical resources found in a hospital?

"If patients are over the age of fifty or have any medical issues at all, we get medical clearance by their physician in writing and appropriate laboratory tests, or we go to the hospital," Dr. Robert Graper, FACS, of Graper Cosmetic Surgery of Charlotte, who performs surgeries in his office and in hospitals, has said.

"When that's the standard of care, I don't think surgery is more dangerous done in an office than a hospital. Some people say it's better, because you don't have all those germs."

By summer 2008 the delays were showing on Sally Hill. She was visibly depressed, not caring about the home she has always loved, decorated and cared for. In fact, she had repairs done and put the house up for sale.

She has sorted through everything in her house—all the memories of her childhood, her teen years, her marriage, her father's death and her mother's numbing Alzheimer's. It was like watching her life flash before her; she could never have imagined that this is where she would find herself at this point in her life.

She put all of her personal belongings in storage. She left the house vacant and moved into the condo that was her parents'. She has remodeled the 60s-style-apartment-turned-condo and it, too, is up for sale.

Friends have become concerned about her deepening depression, which is certainly understandable. Sally has a terrible burden hanging over her head. For her own comfort and for something to nurture, she has been doting on her two remaining cats, one a stray she adopted right before she went to jail. The cats and her aging mother are probably the only way she has of nurturing any living thing these days while she waits to go to trial.

"I just want it to be over," she told a friend who inquired about how she was dealing with the waiting. "I want to move out of Charlotte and bring my mother to live with me," Sally said recently.

"Some days are better than others," she told another friend, saying she works hard to keep her spirits up.

"She was always so jolly, she loved to laugh, and was always really a fun person," said Patty Campbell. "She lost her job, her leukemia that had been in remission returned; she's been punished enough."

While the unconditional love of her cats is no doubt a great comfort to her, Sally has had trouble just providing basic care for them and for herself. She has lost everything—her career, her husband, even her ability to work at all, and, especially hard to accept, her health. In addition she has the unthinkable burden of being charged with murdering a patient still facing her. The question will ultimately be: Was Sandra's death an accident, gross negligence, or deliberate?

All Sally has now is her memories of better times, her deep and constant faith and the endless prayers of her friends and fellow churchgoers.

When all is said and done . . . will that be enough?